MATERIALS FOR
MUSIC FUNDAMENTALS

MATERIALS FOR MUSIC FUNDAMENTALS

Anthology, Rhythmic Reading, and Sight Singing

CHARLES NICK
University of Missouri-Columbia

PRENTICE-HALL, INC.   *Englewood Cliffs, N.J. 07632*

Library of Congress Cataloging in Publication Data

Main entry under title:

Materials for music fundamentals.

    "A source book . . . specifically organized
for courses in fundamentals of music"–Pref.
    1. Music–Theory.   2. Musical meter and
rhythm. 3. Sight-singing. 4. Musical form.
I. Nick, Charles.
MT6.M348 1983   82-16683
ISBN 0-13-560581-4

Editorial/production supervision and interior design: Marion Osterberg
Cover design: Ray Lundgren
Manufacturing buyer: Ray Keating

Printed in the United States of America

10 9 8 7 6 5 4 3 2 1

ISBN 0-13-560581-4

Prentice-Hall International, Inc., *London*
Prentice-Hall of Australia Pty. Limited, *Sydney*
Editora Prentice-Hall do Brasil, Ltda., *Rio de Janeiro*
Prentice-Hall Canada Inc., *Toronto*
Prentice-Hall of India Private Limited, *New Delhi*
Prentice-Hall of Japan, Inc., *Tokyo*
Prentice-Hall of Southeast Asia Pte. Ltd., *Singapore*
Whitehall Books Limited, *Wellington, New Zealand*

Contents

PART I

ANTHOLOGY

1   Simple Meters   **2**

Section A

METER SIGNATURES $\frac{2}{4}$ $\frac{3}{4}$ $\frac{4}{4}$

NOTE VALUES   𝅝   𝅗𝅥.   𝅗𝅥   𝅘𝅥

Section B

METER SIGNATURES $\frac{2}{4}$ $\frac{3}{4}$ $\frac{4}{4}$

ADDITIONAL NOTE VALUES ♩· ♪

Section C

METER SIGNATURES $\frac{2}{4}$ $\frac{3}{4}$ $\frac{4}{4}$

ADDITIONAL NOTE VALUES ♪· ♬

Section D

OTHER SIMPLE METER SIGNATURES $\frac{2}{2}$ ¢ $\frac{3}{2}$ $\frac{4}{2}$ $\frac{3}{8}$

2   Compound Meters   22

Section A

METER SIGNATURES $\frac{6}{8}$ $\frac{9}{8}$ $\frac{12}{8}$

NOTE VALUES

Section B

METER SIGNATURES $\frac{6}{8}$ $\frac{9}{8}$ $\frac{12}{8}$

ADDITIONAL NOTE VALUES

Section C
OTHER COMPOUND METERS $\frac{6}{4}$ $\frac{9}{4}$ $\frac{6}{16}$ $\frac{9}{16}$

3   Major Scales   34

4   Minor Scales   45

5   Harmony in Major Keys   52

6   Harmony in Minor Keys   60

7   Dominant Seventh Chords   69

8   Phrase Structures and Cadences   81

9 Form   96

Section A

BINARY AND ROUNDED BINARY

Section B

SIMPLE AND COMPOUND TERNARY

Section C

RONDO

Section D

SONATA — ALLEGRO

Section E

CONTRAPUNTAL FORMS

RHYTHMIC READING

Preface

Materials for Music Fundamentals is a source book divided into three main parts: (1) Anthology, (II) Rhythmic Reading, (III) Sight Singing. It has been specifically organized for courses in fundamentals of music but may also be used in remedial theory courses for music majors. The anthology includes music from the Renaissance, Baroque, Classic, and Romantic periods and folk songs, carols, hymns, and selections from musicals. The variety of styles and media assures a very broad experience of study. Excerpts are used to illustrate concepts ranging from meters to the dominant seventh chord. In most cases, examples with uncomplicated texture settings have been used to accommodate the development of skills in harmonic, melodic, and structural analysis. Furthermore, the author has harmonized and arranged many of the folk songs to insure a collection of relevant illustrations. Complete movements are utilized for the study of form and have been specifically selected for the exemplary illustration of binary, ternary, rondo, and sonata-allegro forms.

Part II contains original rhythmic exercises in one and two parts. These progress gradually from no division to various subdivisions of the beat. These exercises could be performed on percussion instruments or sung with neutral vowels.

Part III is made up of three units, each of which contains melodies and concludes with duets. The original melodies are first organized with seconds and gradually progress to contours containing major and minor thirds. Comfortable ranges have been applied, and in most cases recorders may be used for the development of reading skills. The choice of singing with numbers, neutral vowels, or syllables is left to the discretion of the instructor.

I am indebted to my students in Fundamentals of Music for providing the initial impetus and motivation to undertake the project of developing this book. Also, I am grateful to my colleagues, Helen K. Harrison, John E. Cheetham, W. Thomas McKenney, and Charles H. Sherman, for their encouragement, advice, and assistance.

Charles Nick

Acknowledgments

MATERIALS FOR
MUSIC FUNDAMENTALS

PART I

ANTHOLOGY

1 Simple Meters

Section A

METER SIGNATURES   **2/4**   **3/4**   **4/4**

NOTE VALUES

(1) **Hymn.** *Fairest Lord Jesus.*

Anonymous in *Munster Gesangbuch*, 1677.
Translator anonymous.

Melody from Schlessiche Volksleider

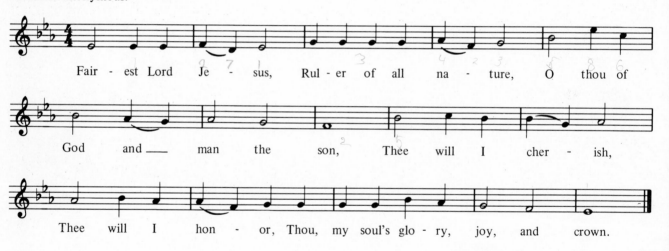

Fair - est Lord Je - sus, Rul - er of all na - ture, O thou of

God and ___ man the son, Thee will I cher - ish,

Thee will I hon - or, Thou, my soul's glo - ry, joy, and crown.

2   **French folk song.** *Sur le pont d'Avignon.*

Allegro

On the bridge (of) A - vi - gnon there is danc - ing, there is danc - ing,

Fine

on the bridge (of) A - vi - gnon there is danc - ing, all a - round.

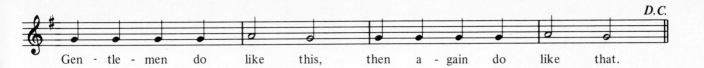

Gen - tle - men do like this, then a - gain do like that.

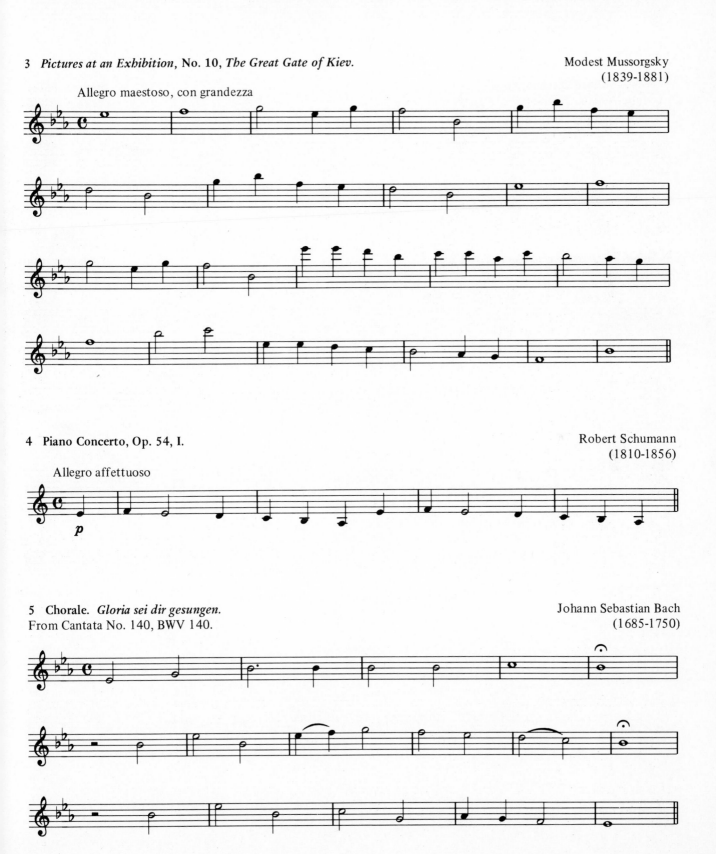

3 *Pictures at an Exhibition*, **No. 10,** *The Great Gate of Kiev.* Modest Mussorgsky
(1839-1881)

Allegro maestoso, con grandezza

4 Piano Concerto, Op. 54, I. Robert Schumann
(1810-1856)

Allegro affettuoso

5 Chorale. *Gloria sei dir gesungen.* Johann Sebastian Bach
From Cantata No. 140, BWV 140. (1685-1750)

6 Symphonic cycle, *My Country*, **No. 2**, *The Moldau.*

Bedřich Smetana
(1824-1884)

Tranquilo

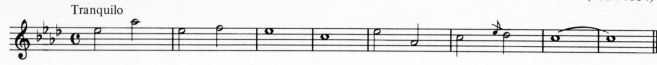

7 *Who Is Sylvia?* **Op. 106, No. 4.**
Words by William Shakespeare (1564-1616).

Franz Schubert
(1797-1828)

Mässig

Who is Syl - via,   what is she — that all our swains com- mend her?

⑧ **Hymn.** *Dear Master, in Whose Life I See.*
Words by John Hunter (1848-1917).

Adapted from
Katholishes Gesangbuch

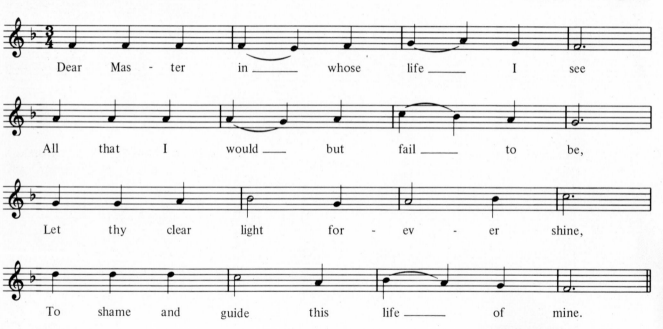

Dear Mas - ter in ___ whose life ___ I see

All that I would ___ but fail ___ to be,

Let thy clear light for - ev - er shine,

To shame and guide this life ___ of mine.

9 Piano Sonata, Op. 27, No. 2, *Moonlight*, II.

Ludwig van Beethoven
(1770-1827)

Allegretto

p

10 *Out of My Dreams.*
From the musical *Oklahoma!* Words by
Oscar Hammerstein II (1895-1960).

Richard Rodgers
(1902-1980)

Out of my dreams and in - to your arms I long

to fly _____ I will come as

eve - ning comes to woo a wait - ing sky. _____

11 Symphony No. 3, Op. 55, I.

Ludwig van Beethoven
(1770-1827)

Allegro con brio

Cello and Bass

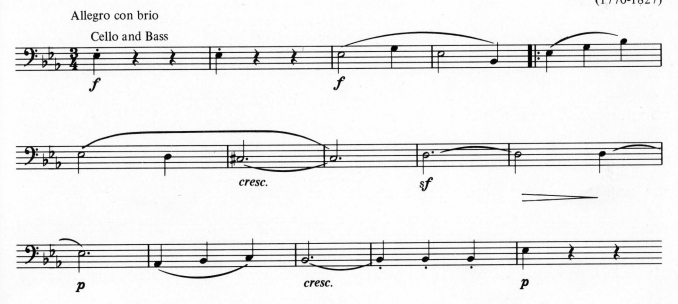

12 Viennese melody.

Andante

13 Polish folk tune.

Pesante

f

mf

(**14**) **Dutch folk tune.**

Andantino

mp

15 Mexican popular tune. *Cielito Lindo.*

Lively .

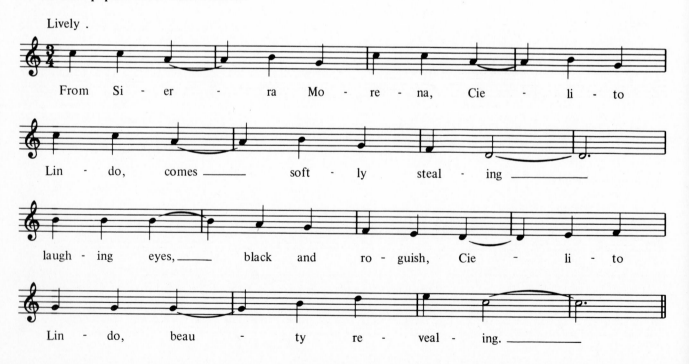

From Si - er - ra Mo - re - na, Cie - li - to

Lin - do, comes ____ soft - ly steal - ing ____

laugh - ing eyes, ____ black and ro - guish, Cie - li - to

Lin - do, beau - ty re - veal - ing. ____

Section B

METER SIGNATURES $\frac{2}{4}$ $\frac{3}{4}$ $\frac{4}{4}$

ADDITIONAL NOTE VALUES ♩. ♪

16 American folk song. *Hush, Little Baby.*

Serenely

Hush, lit - tle ba - by, don't say a word, Dad - dy's gon - na buy you a mock - ing bird.

17 The Sound of Music.
From the musical *The Sound of Music.* Words by
Oscar Hammerstein II (1895-1960).

Richard Rodgers
(1902-1980)

Moderately, with warm expression

p

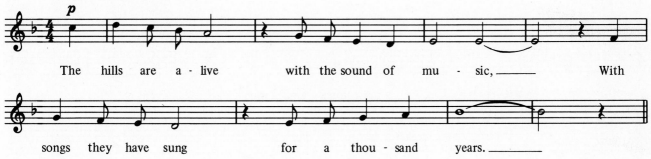

The hills are a - live with the sound of mu - sic,_____ With

songs they have sung for a thou - sand years._____

18 Symphony No. 7, Op. 92, II.

Ludwig van Beethoven
(1770-1827)

Allegretto (♩=76)

ten.

p

19 Hymn. *A Mighty Fortress Is Our God.*
Words by Martin Luther. Translated by
Frederick H. Hedge (1805-1890).

Martin Luther
(1483-1546)

A might - y for - tress is __ our God, A bul - wark nev - er fail - ing;

20 *Do-Re-Mi.*
From the musical *The Sound of Music.*
Words by Oscar Hammerstein II (1895-1960).

Richard Rodgers
(1902-1980)

Brightly

Maria:

Doe a deer, a fe - male deer, Ray a

drop of gold - en sun, _____ Me a name I

call my - self, Far a long, long way to run. _____

Sew a nee - dle pull - ing thread, _____ La, a

note to fol - low sew, _____ Tea a drink with jam and

bread _____ That will bring us back to do - oh - oh - oh!

21 *Climb Ev'ry Mountain.*
From the musical *The Sound of Music.* Words by
Oscar Hammerstein II (1895-1960).

Richard Rodgers
(1902-1980)

Maestoso

Refrain (with deep feeling, like a prayer)

Climb ev - 'ry moun - tain, search high and low,

8 Anthology

Fol - low ev - 'ry by - way, ev - 'ry path you know.

22 *If with All Your Hearts.* Felix Mendelssohn
From the oratorio *Elijah,* No. 4. (1809-1847)

Andante con moto (♩=72)

"If with all your hearts ye tru - ly seek me,

ye shall ev - er sure - ly find me." Thus saith our God,

23 Russian folk song. *Lovely Minka.*

Moderato

mf

24 Symphony No. 5, Op. 95, *The New World,* IV. Antonin Dvořák
(1841-1904)

Allegro con fuoco

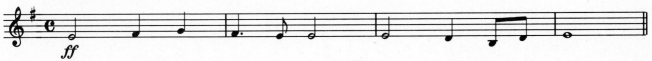

ff

25 Italian melody.

Allegretto

26 American chantey. *Shenandoah.*

Expressively

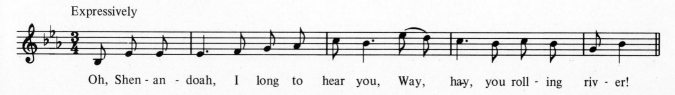

Oh, Shen - an - doah, I long to hear you, Way, hay, you roll - ing riv - er!

27 Motet: *Exsultate Jubilate*, **K 165, III,** *Alleluja.*

Wolfgang Amadeus Mozart
(1756-1791)

Al - le - lu - ja, al - le - lu - ja, _____

al - le - lu - ja, al - le - lu - ja.

28 Piano Sonata, K 332, I.

Wolfgang Amadeus Mozart
(1756-1791)

29 *I've Grown Accustomed to Her Face.*
From the musical *My Fair Lady*. Words by
Alan Jay Lerner (1918-   ).

Frederick Loewe
(1904-   )

I've grown ac - cus-tomed to her   face _____   She al-most makes the day be - gin. _____   I've grown ac-

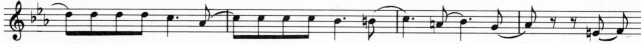

cus-tomed to   the tune   she whist - les night and noon, Her smile, her frowns, her ups,   her downs,

30 *Oklahoma.*
From the musical *Oklahoma*. Words by
Oscar Hammerstein II (1895-1960).

Richard Rodgers
(1902-1980)

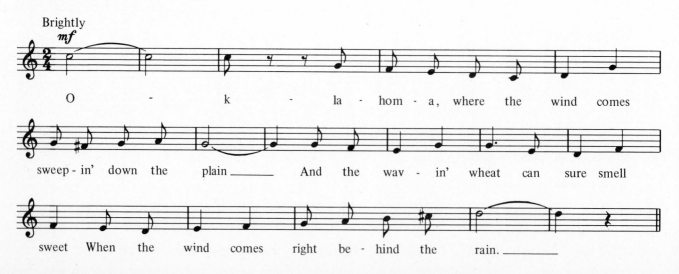

O   -   k   -   la - hom - a,   where   the   wind   comes

sweep - in' down   the   plain _____   And   the   wav - in' wheat   can   sure   smell

sweet When   the   wind   comes   right   be - hind   the   rain. _____

31 *Try to Remember.*
From the musical *Fantasticks.* Words by
Tom Jones (1928-   ).

Harvey Schmidt
(1929-   )

Moderato

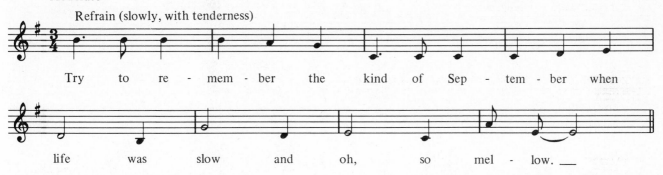

Try to re - mem - ber the kind of Sep - tem - ber when

life was slow and oh, so mel - low. ___

Section C

METER SIGNATURES $\frac{2}{4}$ $\frac{3}{4}$ $\frac{4}{4}$

ADDITIONAL NOTE VALUES

32 French folk song. *Frère Jacques.*

Modéré

Frè - re Jac - ques, frè - re Jac - ques, Dor - mez - vous? dor - mez - vous?

Son - nez les ma - tin - es, son - nez les ma - tin - es, Din din, don; din, din, don.

33 *And He Shall Purify.*
From the oratorio *Messiah.*

George Frideric Handel
(1685-1759)

Allegro (♩=72)

Soprano

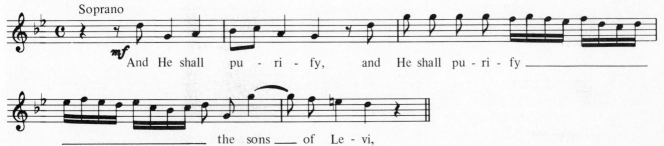

mf
And He shall pu - ri - fy, and He shall pu - ri - fy _____

_____ the sons ___ of Le - vi,

34 String Quartet, Op. 64, No. 5, *The Lark*, IV.

Franz Joseph Haydn
(1732-1809)

Finale

Vivace

35 Concerto Grosso, Op. 3, No. 6, I.

Antonio Vivaldi
(1675-1741)

Allegro

36 *When I Was a Lad*.
From the musical *H.M.S. Pinafore*. Words by
William S. Gilbert (1836-1911).

Arthur S. Sullivan
(1842-1900)

Lightly

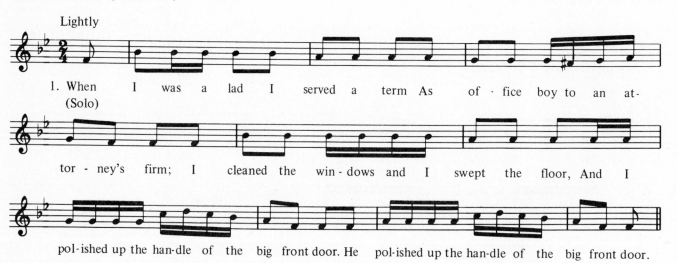

1. When   I   was   a   lad   I   served   a   term   As   of - fice   boy   to   an   at-
(Solo)

tor - ney's   firm;   I   cleaned   the   win - dows   and   I   swept   the   floor,   And   I

pol - ished up the han - dle of the big front door. He   pol - ished up the han - dle of the big front door.

37 Old American tune.

Andante

38 Opera. *Carmen*, **Prelude to Act I.**

Georges Bizet
(1838-1875)

Allegro giocoso (♩=116)

39 Organ Fugue in G Minor ("Little"), BWV 578.

Johann Sebastian Bach
(1685-1750)

40 American song. *I've Been Working on the Railroad.*

March tempo

I've   been work - ing   on   the   rail - road   all   the   live - long   day;

I've   been work - ing   on   the   rail - road   to   pass   the   time   a - way.

Don't   you   hear the whis - tle   blow - ing;   Rise   up   so ear - ly   in the morn.

Don't   you   hear   the cap - tain   shout - ing,   "Di - nah, blow your   horn!"

41 Symphony No. 100, *Military, Menuetto*, Hob. I:100.

Franz Joseph Haydn
(1732-1809)

Moderato

42 *Let Me Entertain You.*
From the musical *Gypsy*. Words by Stephen Sondheim (1930-   ).

Jule Styne
(1905-   )

Moderato

Refrain (with a lilt and not fast)

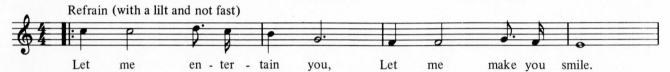

Let   me   en - ter - tain   you,   Let   me   make you smile.

Let me do   a few tricks, some old and then some new tricks, I'm ver - y   ver - sa - tile.

43 *Minuetto.*
From the opera *Don Giovanni*, K 527.

Wolfgang Amadeus Mozart
(1756-1791)

Minuetto

44 Symphony No. 5, Op. 107, *Reformation*, II.

Felix Mendelssohn
(1809-1847)

Allegro vivace

45 *Jingle Bells.*

James Pierpont
(1822-1893)

Allegro

Jin - gle bells, Jin - gle bells, Jin - gle all the way, Oh, what fun it is to ride in a

one-horse o - pen sleigh! __ Jin - gle bells, Jin - gle bells, Jin - gle all the way,

Oh, what fun it is to ride in a one-horse o - pen sleigh!

46 Folk song from southern United States. *Skip to My Lou.*

Lively

Fly in the but - ter - milk, shoo fly shoo! Fly in the but - ter - milk, shoo fly, shoo!

Fly in the but - ter - milk, shoo fly, shoo! Skip to my Lou my dar - ling.

47 English folk song. *Frog Went A-courtin'.*

Allegro

A frog went a - court - in' and he did ride, __ uh, huh! A

frog went a - court - in' and he did ride, __ uh, huh! A

frog went a - court - in' and he did ride, __ Sword and pis - tol by his side, __ uh, huh!

48 Symphony No. 5, Op. 95, *From the New World*, I.

Antonin Dvořák
(1841-1904)

Allegro molto

Section D

OTHER SIMPLE METER SIGNATURES $\frac{2}{2}$ ¢ $\frac{3}{2}$ $\frac{4}{2}$ $\frac{3}{8}$

49 Hymn. *Let All Mortal Flesh Keep Silence.*
Liturgy of St. James. Translated by Gerard
Moultrie (1829-1885).

Traditional
French melody

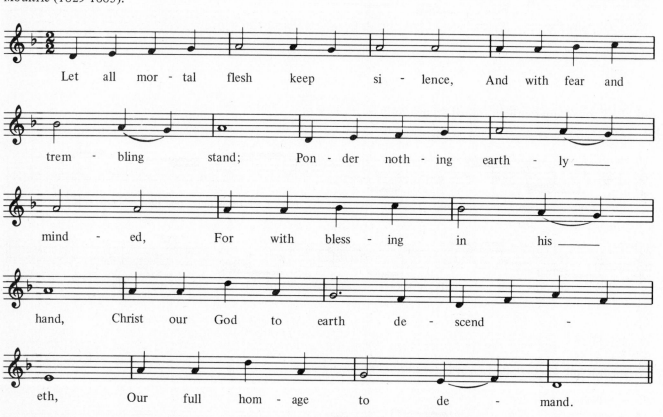

Let all mor - tal flesh keep si - lence, And with fear and

trem - bling stand; Pon - der noth - ing earth - ly _____

mind - ed, For with bless - ing in his _____

hand, Christ our God to earth de - scend -

eth, Our full hom - age to de - mand.

50 French carol. *Pat-a-pan.*

Marchlike

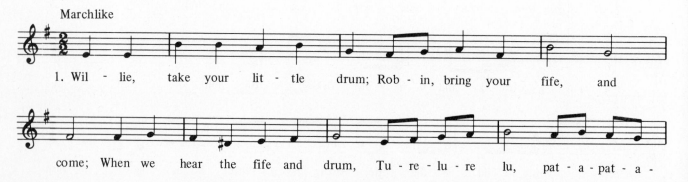

1. Wil - lie, take your lit - tle drum; Rob - in, bring your fife, and

come; When we hear the fife and drum, Tu - re - lu - re lu, pat - a - pat - a -

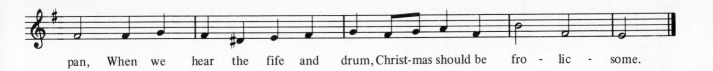

pan, When we hear the fife and drum, Christ-mas should be fro - lic - some.

51 American folk song. *Little 'Liza Jane.*

Briskly

You got a gal and I got none, Lit - tle Li - za Jane;

Come my love and be my one, Lit - tle Li - za Jane.

52 American folk song. *A Hot Time in the Old Town.*

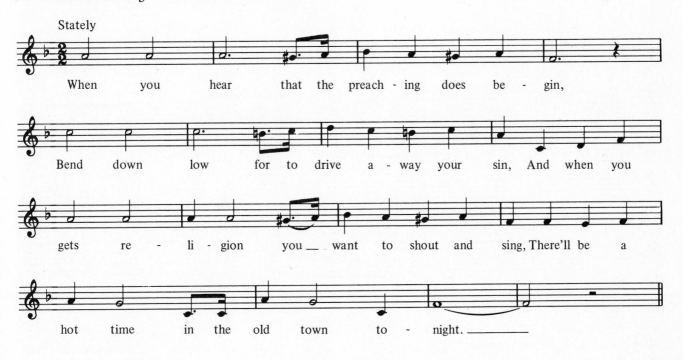

Stately

When you hear that the preach - ing does be - gin,

Bend down low for to drive a - way your sin, And when you

gets re - li - gion you __ want to shout and sing, There'll be a

hot time in the old town to - night. _____

53 Overture.
From the opera *I Promessi Sposi.*

Amilcare Ponchielli
(1834-1886)

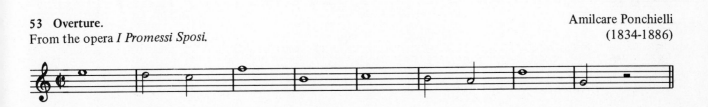

54 Organ chorale. *Vater unser in Himmelreich.*

Ulrich Steigleder
(1593-1635)

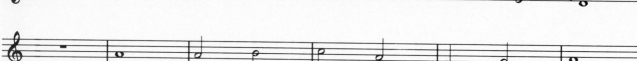

55 New Orleans processional. *When the Saints Go Marching In.*

March tempo

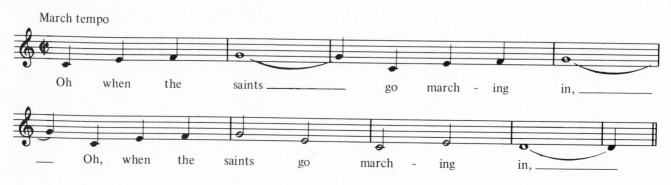

Oh   when   the   saints _____ go march - ing   in, _____

— Oh, when   the   saints   go   march - ing   in, _____

56 March. *The Thunderer.*

John Philip Sousa
(1854-1932)

March tempo

57 *Deploration sur la mort Okeghem.*

Josquin des Prez
(1440-1521)

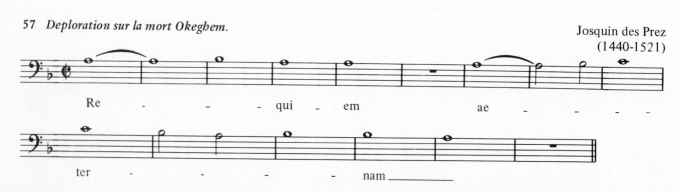

Re - - qui - em   ae - - - -

ter - - - - nam _____

58 Southern folk song. *Mister Banjo.*

Sprightly

Look at the dan-dy there, Mis-ter Ban-jo, Does-n't he put on airs,

Hat cocked on one side, Mis-ter Ban-jo, Walk-in' stick in han',

Look at the dan-dy there, Mis-ter Ban-jo, Does-n't he put on airs.

59 German Christmas song.

60 Symphony No. 9, Op. 125, IV.

Ludwig van Beethoven
(1770-1827)

Andante maestoso (♩=72)

61 Spiritual. *Goin' Over Jordan.*

Broadly

62 Chaconne.

Giovanni Battista Vitali
(1632-1692)

Moderato

f

63 Hymn. *Jesus, Lover of My Soul.*
Words by Charles Wesley (1707-1788).

Joseph Parry
(1841-1903)

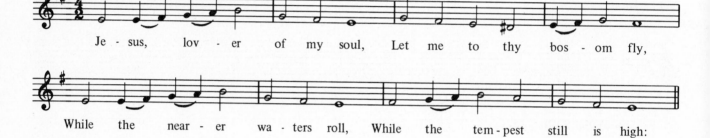

Je - sus,   lov - er   of   my   soul,   Let   me   to   thy   bos - om   fly,

While   the   near - er   wa - ters   roll,   While   the   tem - pest   still   is   high:

64 French folk song.

Allegro

mf

65 French carol. *Bring a Torch, Jeannette, Isabella.*

Allegretto

Bring   a   torch,____   Jean - nette,   Is - a - bel - la,   Bring   a

torch __ and quick - ly run. Christ is born, __ good

folk of the vil - lage, Christ __ is born and Ma - ry's

call - ing, Ah! ah! beau - ti - ful is the

Moth - er, Ah! ah! beau - ti - ful is Her Son.

66 Trio for Piano, Violin, and Cello, K 564, II.

Wolfgang Amadeus Mozart
(1756-1791)

Andante

67 Neapolitan serenade. *Santa Lucia.*
Translated by Thomas Oliphant.

Teodoro Cottrau
(1827-1879)

Amorously

Now 'neath the sil - ver moon, o - cean is glow - ing,

O'er the calm bil - low, soft winds are blow - ing.

68 String Quartet, Op. 18, No. 4, II.

Ludwig van Beethoven
(1770-1827)

Andante scherzoso quasi allegretto

pp

2 Compound Meters

Section A

METER SIGNATURES $\frac{6}{8}$ $\frac{9}{8}$ $\frac{12}{8}$

NOTE VALUES

69 Fourteenth century German melody.
Good Christian Men, Rejoice.
Paraphrase by John Neale (1818-1866).

In Dulci Jubilo

Good Chris - tian men, re - joice ____ With heart and soul and

voice; ____ Give ye heed to what we say: News! News! Je - sus Christ is

born to - day: Ox and ass be - fore Him bow, And He is in the

man - ger now; Christ is born to - day! ___ Christ is born to - day!

70 *Hey, Look Me Over.*
From the musical *Wildcat.* Words by Carolyn Leigh (1926-   ).

Cy Coleman
(1929-   )

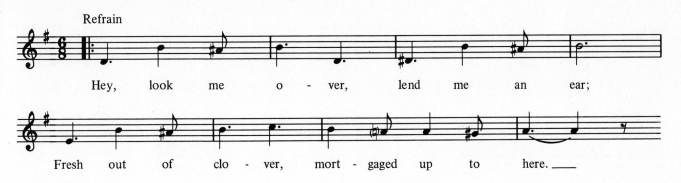

Hey,   look   me   o - ver,   lend   me   an   ear;

Fresh   out   of   clo - ver,   mort - gaged   up   to   here. ___

71 *Funiculi, Funicula.*

Luigi Denza
(1846-1922)

Some   think ___   the world   is   made   for   fun   and   frol - lic, ___

___ And   so   do   I! ___   And   so   do   I! ___

72 English folk song. *The Farmer in the Dell.*

The   farm - er   in   the   dell, ___   the   farm - er   in   the   dell,

Hi!   ho!   the   der - ry   oh,   the   farm - er   in   the   dell. ___

73 March. *Washington Post.*

John Philip Sousa
(1854-1932)

74 Traditional English song. *I Saw Three Ships.*

Allegro

I saw three ships come sail - ing in, On Christ - mas Day, on Christ - mas Day; I

saw three ships come sail - ing in, On Christ - mas Day in the morn - ing.

75 American Chantey. *Good-by, My Lover, Good-by.*

Moderato

1. The ship is sail - ing down the bay, good - by, my lov - er, good - by;___ We
2. My heart will ev - er - more be true, good - by, my lov - er, good - by;___ Tho'

may not meet for man - y a day, good - by, my lov - er, good - by!___
now we sad - ly say a - dieu, good - by, my lov - er, good - by!___

Refrain

By - low, my ba - by, by - low, my ba - by,

By - low, my ba - by, good - by, my lov - er, good - by!___

76 Folk song from the British Isles. *The Devil and the Farmer's Wife.*

Spirited

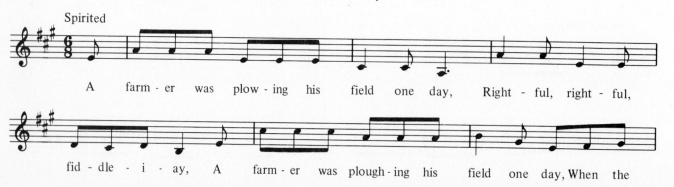

A farm - er was plow - ing his field one day, Right - ful, right - ful,

fid - dle - i - ay, A farm - er was plough - ing his field one day, When the

dev - il came up and to him he did say, "With my right - ful, right - ful,

fid - dle - i - ay, With my right - ful fid - dle - i - ay."____

77 String Quartet, K 589, IV.

Wolfgang Amadeus Mozart
(1756-1791)

Allegro assai

p

78 Symphony No. 3, Op. 56, *Scotch*, I.

Felix Mendelssohn
(1809-1847)

Allegro un poco agitato (♩=100)

79 Horn Concerto, K 447, III.

Wolfgang Amadeus Mozart
(1756-1791)

Allegro

p

80 Symphony No. 101, Hob. I:101, I.

Franz Joseph Haydn
(1732-1809)

Presto

81 *Beautiful Dreamer.*

Stephen Foster
(1826-1864)

Moderato

Beau - ti - ful dream - er, wake un - to me,____ Mer - maids are chant - ing the wild lo - re - lie; ____

82 Cantata No. 147, *Jesu Joy of Man's Desiring*, BWV 147:6.

Johann Sebastian Bach
(1685-1750)

83 Southern United States folk song. *Down in the Valley.*

Down in the val - ley the val - ley so low, Hang your head o - ver, hear the wind blow.

84 Two-Part Invention, No. 10, BWV 781.

Johann Sebastian Bach
(1685-1750)

85 Round. *Three Blind Mice.*
Mother Goose rhyme.

Animated

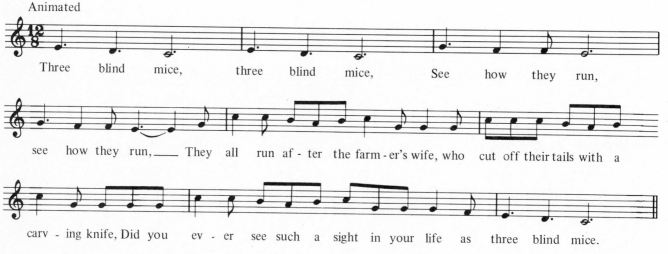

Three   blind   mice,   three   blind   mice,   See   how   they   run,

see   how they run,____ They   all   run af - ter   the farm - er's wife, who   cut off their tails with a

carv - ing knife, Did you   ev - er   see such   a   sight in your life   as   three   blind   mice.

86 Partie (Partita), Gigue.

Johann N. Tischer
(1707- ?)

Presto assai

87 Symphony No. 5, Op. 64, II.

Peter Ilyich Tchaikovsky
(1840-1893)

Andante cantabile

88 Suite No. 4, for Piano, 5th Movement, Gigue.

George Frideric Handel
(1685-1759)

89 American song. *Looby Loo.*

Here   we   go   loo - by   loo,   Here   we   go   loo - by   light,

Here   we   go   loo - by   loo,   all   on   a   Sat - ur - day   night.

Section B

METER SIGNATURES **6/8   9/8   12/8**

ADDITIONAL NOTE VALUES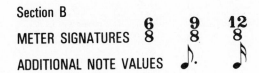

90 Concerto Grosso, Op. 3, No. 10, *L'Estro Armonico,* **III.**

Antonio Vivaldi
(1675-1741)

Allegro

II Violin

91 English folk song, *Lavender's Blue.* A A'

Merrily

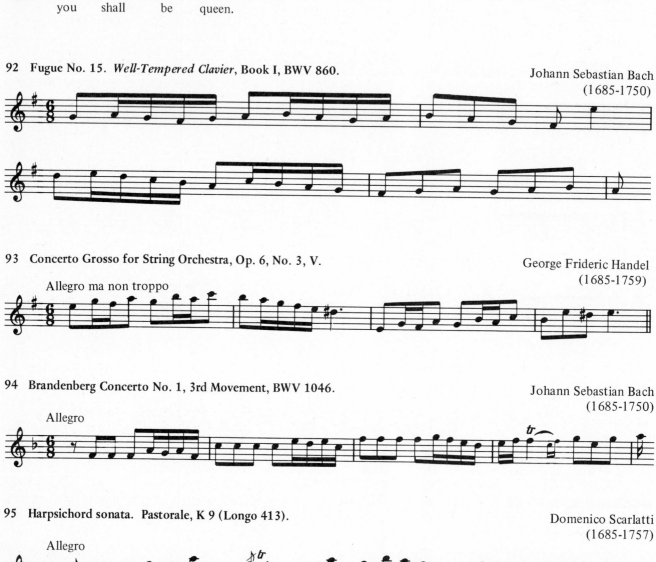

1. Lav - en - der's blue, dil - ly, dil - ly, lav - en - der's green, When I am king, dil - ly, dil - ly,

you shall be queen.

92 Fugue No. 15. *Well-Tempered Clavier*, Book I, BWV 860.

Johann Sebastian Bach
(1685-1750)

93 Concerto Grosso for String Orchestra, Op. 6, No. 3, V.

George Frideric Handel
(1685-1759)

Allegro ma non troppo

94 Brandenberg Concerto No. 1, 3rd Movement, BWV 1046.

Johann Sebastian Bach
(1685-1750)

Allegro

95 Harpsichord sonata. Pastorale, K 9 (Longo 413).

Domenico Scarlatti
(1685-1757)

Allegro

96 Concerto for Clarinet, K 622, III.

Wolfgang Amadeus Mozart
(1756-1791)

Allegro

97 *Goldberg Variations, No. 24, BWV 988.*

Johann Sebastian Bach
(1685-1750)

98 Partita for Pianoforte, No. 5, Gigue, BWV 829.

Johann Sebastian Bach
(1685-1750)

99 Christmas carol. *Silent Night.*

Franz Gruber
(1787-1863)

Si - lent night, ho - ly night, All is calm, all is bright,

Round yon vir - gin moth - er and child. Ho - ly in - fant so ten - der and mild,

100 Mother Goose rhyme. *Little Boy Blue.*   A B

Gently

Lit - tle Boy Blue come blow your horn, The sheep's in the mead - ow, the cow's in the corn;

Where is the boy who looks aft - er the sheep? He's un - der the hay - stack fast a - sleep.

101 *How Beautiful Are the Feet.*
From the oratorio *Messiah.*

George Frideric Handel
(1685-1759)

Larghetto (♪=104)

mp

102 Irish folk song. *Believe Me, If All Those Endearing Young Charms.*
Words by Thomas Moore (1779-1852).

Flowing

Be - lieve me if all those en - dear-ing young charms, which I gaze on so fond - ly to - day__ were to

change by to - mor - row and fleet in my arms, Like__ fair - y gifts fad - ing a - way.__

103 *Devils Trill.*
For violin and piano.

Giuseppe Tartini
(1692-1770)

104 Pastoral Symphony.
From the oratorio *Messiah.*

George Frideric Handel
(1685-1759)

Larghetto (♪ =132)

mp

Section C
OTHER COMPOUND METERS $\frac{6}{4}$ $\frac{9}{4}$ $\frac{6}{16}$ $\frac{9}{16}$

105 Organ chorale. *Komm, heiliger Geist, Herre Gott.*

Matthias Weckmann
(1621-1674)

106 Hymn. *Jesus, Keep Me Near the Cross.*
Words by Fanny J. Crosby (1820-1915).

Je - sus, keep me near the cross; There a pre - cious foun - tain,

Free to all, a heal - ing stream, Flow's from Cal - vary's moun - tain.

107 Die Lotosblume. *Myrthen*, Op. 25, No. 7.

Robert Schumann
(1810-1856)

Ziemlich langsam

p

Die Lo - tos - blu - me äng - stigt

sich vor der Son - ne Pracht, und mit ge - senk - tem Haup - te er -

war - tet sie träumend die Nacht. Der Mond der ist ___ ihr Buh - le,

108 Liebestraum No. 3 for Piano.

Franz Liszt
(1811-1886)

Poco allegro

109 British ballad. *Scarborough Fair.*

Are you go - ing to Scar - bo - rough Fair? Pars - ley, sage, rose -

mar - y, and thyme. Re - mem - ber me to one that lives there. ___ For

she once was a true love of mine.

110 *The Queen's Command.*
For Harpsichord.

Orlando Gibbons
(1583-1625)

111 Old English song.

112 Ballade, No. 1, Op. 23.

Frédéric Chopin
(1810-1849)

113 Prelude No. 4, *Well-Tempered Clavier,*
Book I, BWV 849.

Johann Sebastian Bach
(1685-1750)

114 Hymn. *Have Thine Own Way, Lord.*
Words by Adelaide A. Pollard (1862-1934).

George C. Stebbins
(1846-1945)

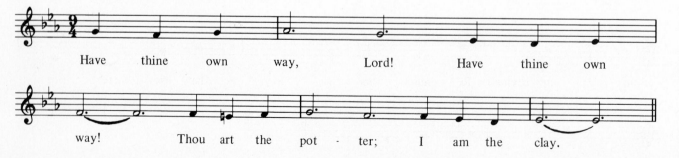

Have thine own way, Lord! Have thine own

way! Thou art the pot - ter; I am the clay.

115 Fugue No. 11, *Well-Tempered Clavier,*
Book II, BWV 880.

Johann Sebastian Bach
(1685-1750)

116 Partita No. 4, Gigue, BWV 828.

Johann Sebastian Bach
(1685-1750)

3 Major Scales

117 Easter hymn. *Christ the Lord Is Risen Today.*
Words by Charles Wesley (1707-1788) *et al.*

Music from *Lyra Davidica*
1708

Christ the Lord is risen to-day,___ Al - le - lu - ia!

Sons of men and an-gels say,___ Al - le - lu - ia!

118 Christmas carol. *O Come, All Ye Faithful.*
Translated by Frederick Oakley (1802-1880) *et al.*

John F. Wade
(1710-1786)

Refrain

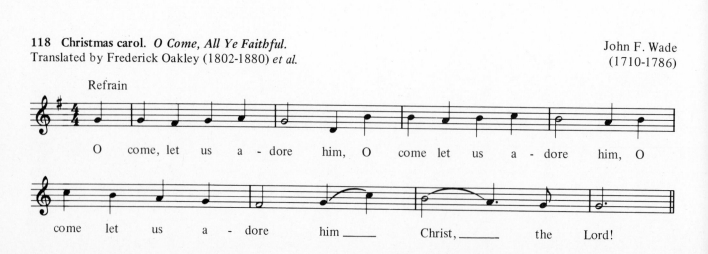

O come, let us a - dore him, O come let us a - dore him, O

come let us a - dore him ___ Christ, ___ the Lord!

119 Hymn. *Let Us Break Bread Together.*

American folk hymn

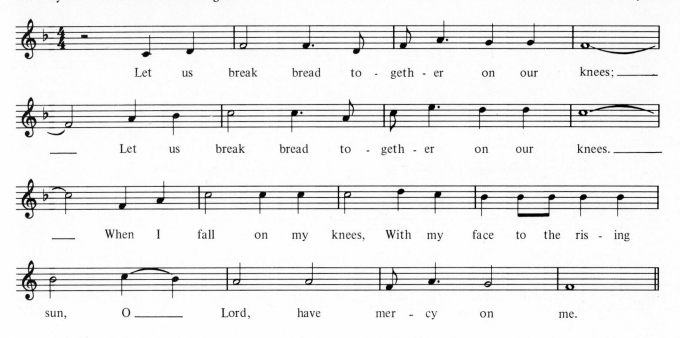

Let us break bread to - geth - er on our knees;____

____ Let us break bread to - geth - er on our knees.____

____ When I fall on my knees, With my face to the ris - ing

sun, O ____ Lord, have mer - cy on me.

120 Symphony No. 94, *Surprise,* Menuet, Hob. I:94.

Franz Joseph Haydn
(1732-1809)

121 Spiritual. *Balm in Gilead.*

There is a balm in Gil - le - ad, to make the wound - ed

whole,— There is a balm in Gi - le - ad, to heal the sin sick soul.

122 American military song. *Marine's Hymn.*

Briskly

From the Halls of Mon - te - zu - ma To the shores of Trip - o - li; _____ We ____ fight our coun - try's bat - tles In the air, on land and sea; _____ First to fight for right and free - dom And to keep our hon - or clean; _____ We are proud to claim the ti - tle Of U - nit - ed States Ma - rine. _____

123 Spiritual. *Nobody Knows the Trouble I've Seen.*

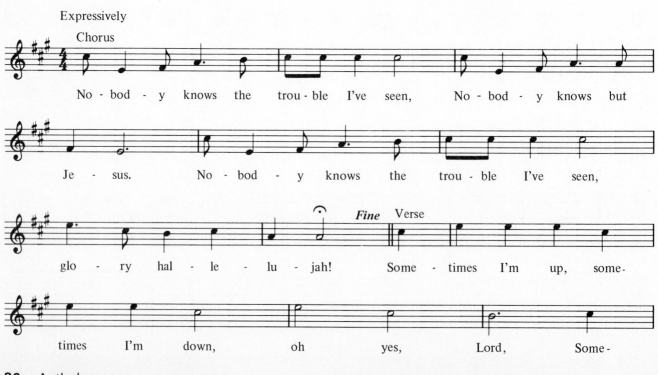

Expressively

Chorus

No - bod - y knows the trou - ble I've seen, No - bod - y knows but Je - sus. No - bod - y knows the trou - ble I've seen, glo - ry hal - le - lu - jah! Some - times I'm up, some-

Fine Verse

times I'm down, oh yes, Lord, Some-

times I'm al - most to the ground, oh yes, Lord.

124 Christmas carol. *Away in a Manger.*
Anonymous.

James R. Murray
(1841-1905)

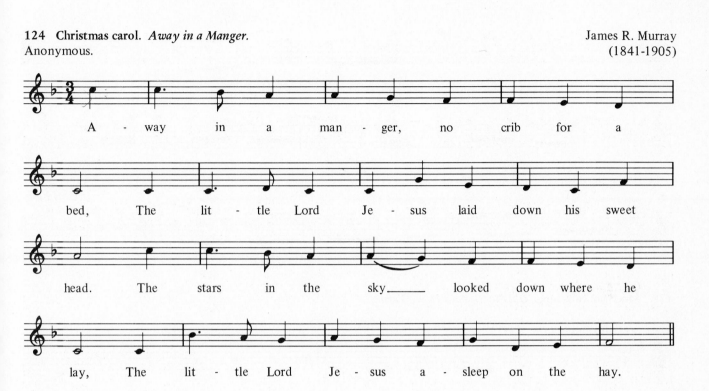

A - way in a man - ger, no crib for a

bed, The lit - tle Lord Je - sus laid down his sweet

head. The stars in the sky___ looked down where he

lay, The lit - tle Lord Je - sus a - sleep on the hay.

125 *Hello, Young Lovers.*
From the musical *The King and I.* Words by
Oscar Hammerstein II (1895-1960).

Richard Rodgers
(1902-1980)

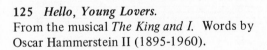

Refrain (Very moderately)

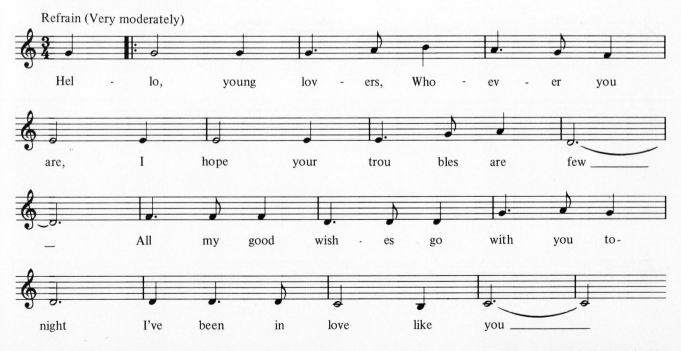

Hel - lo, young lov - ers, Who - ev - er you

are, I hope your trou - bles are few _____

___ All my good wish - es go with you to-

night I've been in love like you _____

126 Piano Concerto, K 482, III.

Wolfgang Amadeus Mozart
(1756-1791)

127 American folk song. *Old MacDonald Had a Farm.*

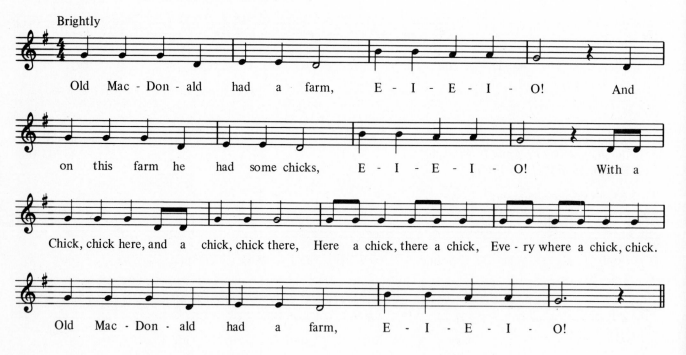

Old Mac - Don - ald had a farm, E - I - E - I - O! And

on this farm he had some chicks, E - I - E - I - O! With a

Chick, chick here, and a chick, chick there, Here a chick, there a chick, Eve - ry where a chick, chick.

Old Mac - Don - ald had a farm, E - I - E - I - O!

128 Spiritual. *Every Time I Feel the Spirit.*

Eve - ry time I ____ feel the spir - it ____ mov - ing

in my heart ___ I will pray. Eve - ry time I ___ feel the

spir - it ___ mov - ing in my heart ___ I will pray.

129 Vier Impromptu, Op. 142, II.   Franz Schubert
                                                                    (1797-1828)

Allegretto

sempre ligato

130 *I Cain't Say No.*   Richard Rodgers
From the musical *Oklahoma!* Words by   (1902-1980)
Oscar Hammerstein II (1895-1960).

Refrain
mp

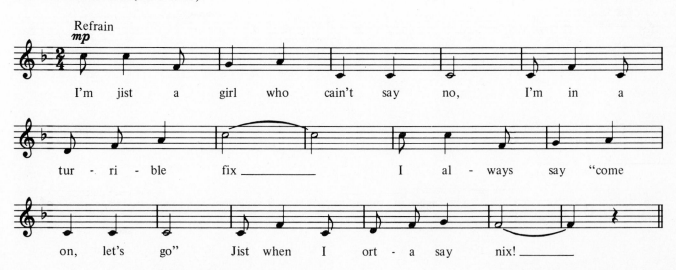

I'm jist a girl who cain't say no, I'm in a

tur - ri - ble fix ___ I al - ways say "come

on, let's go" Jist when I ort - a say nix! ___

131 English game song. *London Bridge.*

Lon - don Bridge is fall - ing down, Fall - ing down, fall - ing down,

Lon - don Bridge is fall - ing down, My fair La - dy.

132 *Habanera.*
From the opera *Carmen,* Act I, No. 5.

Georges Bizet
(1838-1875)

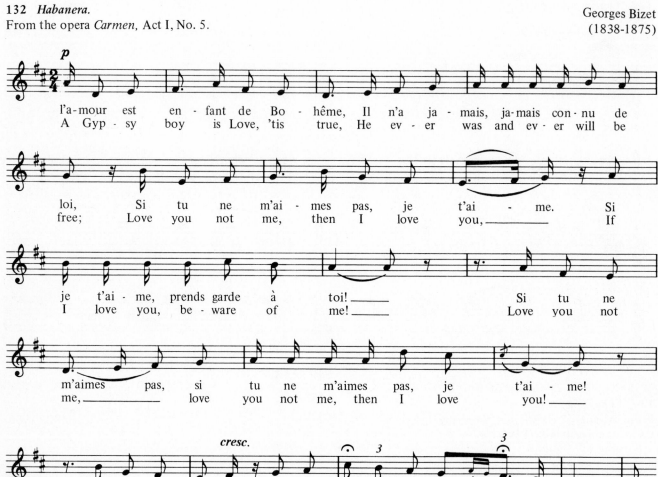

p

l'a-mour est en - fant de Bo - hême, Il n'a ja - mais, ja - mais con - nu de
A Gyp - sy boy is Love, 'tis true, He ev - er was and ev - er will be

loi, Si tu ne m'ai - mes pas, je t'ai - me. Si
free; Love you not me, then I love you,_____ If

je t'ai - me, prends garde à toi! _____ Si tu ne
I love you, be - ware of me! _____ Love you not

m'aimes pas, si tu ne m'aimes pas, je t'ai - me!
me,_____ love you not me, then I love you! _____

cresc.

Mais si je t'aime, si je t'ai - me, prends garde_____ à toi!
But if I love you, if I love you, Be - ware_____ of me!

133 *Schöne Fremde (Fair Far Land).*
From *Liederkreis,* Op. 39, No. 6.

Robert Schumann
(1810-1856)

Innig, bewegt

p

Es fun - keln auf nich al - le Ster - ne mit glü - hen dem Lie - bes-

blick,   es re - det trun - ken die Fer - ne wie von

künf - ti - gem gro - ssen Glück!

134 Spiritual. *All Night, All Day.*

Decisively

All   night,   all _____ day,   An - gels watch - ing o - ver me, my Lord __

Fine

All   night,   all _____ day,   An - gels watch - ing o - ver me.

Now   I lay me   down _ to sleep,   An - gels watch - ing o - ver me, my Lord __

D.C.

Pray   the Lord my   soul _ to keep,   An - gels watch - ing o - ver me.

135 Ländler, Op. 18, No. 3.

Franz Schubert
(1797-1828)

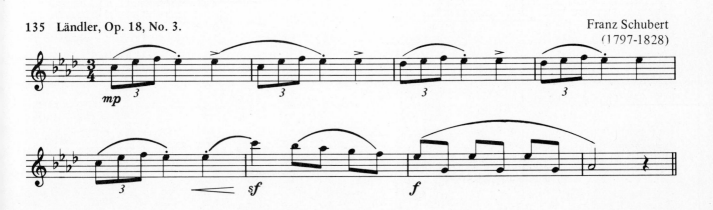

136 *Weigenleid (Cradle Song),* **Op. 49, No. 4**
(Original key, E♭)

Johannes Brahms
(1833-1897)

Zart bewegt

Gu - ten A - bend, gut' Nacht, mit Ro - sen be -

dacht, mit Näg - lein be - steckt schlüpf' un - ter die

Deck': Mor - gen früh, wenn Gott will, wirst du wie - der ge -

weckt, mor - gen früh, wenn Gott will, wirst du wie - der ge - weckt.

137 **Symphony No. 5, 4th Movement.**

Franz Schubert
(1797-1828)

Allegro vivace

138 **Ländler, Op. 18, No. 11.**

Franz Schubert
(1797-1828)

p

139 **English folk song.** *Billy Boy.*

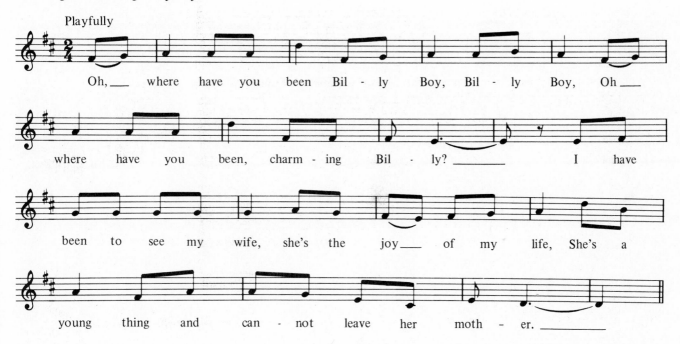

Oh,___ where have you been Bil - ly Boy, Bil - ly Boy, Oh___

where have you been, charm - ing Bil - ly? _____ I have

been to see my wife, she's the joy___ of my life, She's a

young thing and can - not leave her moth - er. _____

140 *Every Valley.*
From the oratorio *Messiah.*

George Frideric Handel
(1685-1759)

Ev - 'ry val - ley, ev 'ry val - ley ___

___ shall be ex - alt - ed, shall be _____ ex - alt - -

- - - - - - - - - - - - -

- - - - - - - - - - - - - ed,

Franz Joseph Haydn
(1756-1809)

4 Minor Scales

142 Spiritual. *Wayfaring Stranger*.

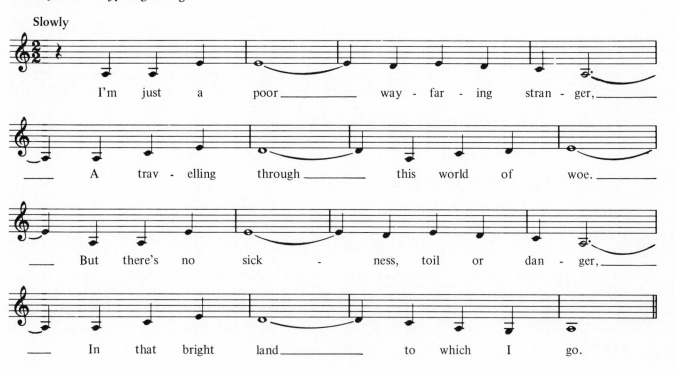

Slowly

I'm just a poor _____ way - far - ing stran - ger, _____

_____ A trav - elling through _____ this world of woe. _____

_____ But there's no sick - ness, toil or dan - ger, _____

_____ In that bright land _____ to which I go.

143 American Chantey. *Drunken Sailor*.

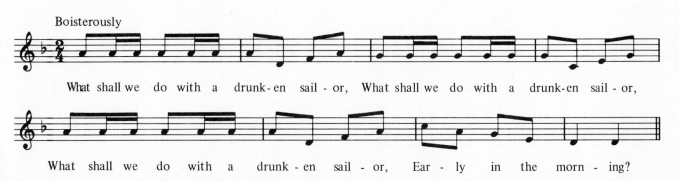

Boisterously

What shall we do with a drunk - en sail - or, What shall we do with a drunk - en sail - or,

What shall we do with a drunk - en sail - or, Ear - ly in the morn - ing?

144 *Summertime.*
From the musical *Porgy and Bess.*
Words by DuBose Heyward (1885-1940).

George Gershwin
(1898-1937)

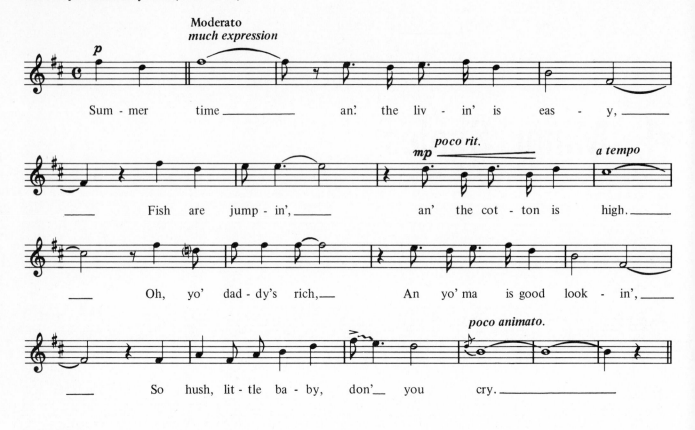

Sum - mer time _____ an' the liv - in' is eas - y, _____

_____ Fish are jump - in', _____ an' the cot - ton is high. _____

Oh, yo' dad - dy's rich, _____ An yo' ma is good look - in', _____

_____ So hush, lit - tle ba - by, don' you cry. _____

145 **English folk song.** *The Tailor and the Mouse.*

Playfully

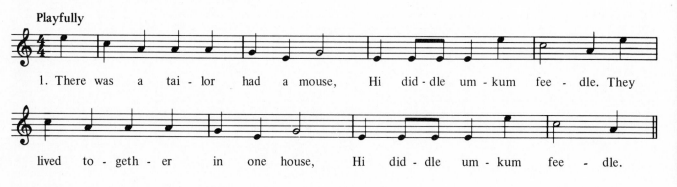

1. There was a tai - lor had a mouse, Hi did - dle um - kum fee - dle. They

lived to - geth - er in one house, Hi did - dle um - kum fee - dle.

146 **Hymn.** *O Come, O Come, Emmanuel.*
Translated by John M. Neale (1818-1866).

Adapted from *Plainsong*
by Thomas Helmore
(1811-1890)

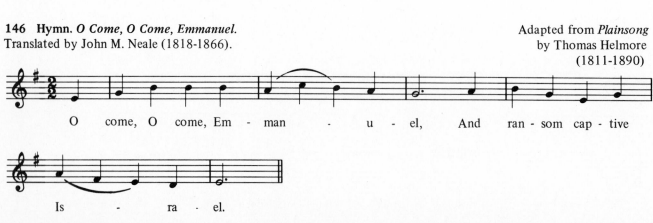

O come, O come, Em - man - u - el, And ran - som cap - tive

Is - ra - el.

147 Ukrainian melody.

Brilliant

148 Children's Songs, Op. 54, No. 5, *Legend*.

Peter Ilyich Tchaikovsky
(1840-1893)

Moderato

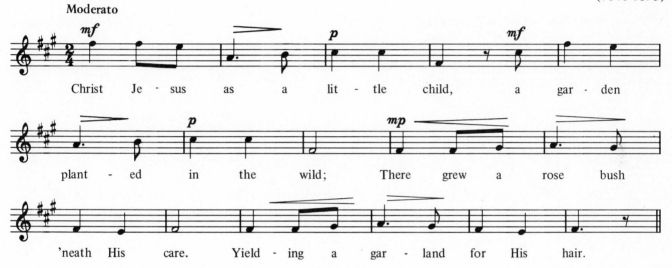

Christ Je - sus as a lit - tle child, a gar - den

plant - ed in the wild; There grew a rose bush

'neath His care. Yield - ing a gar - land for His hair.

149 O Help Me! O Help Me!
From the opera *Magic Flute*, Act I, No. 1, Introduction.

Wolfgang Amadeus Mozart
(1756-1791)

Allegro

Zu Hül - fe! zu Hül - fe! sonst bin ich ver - lo - ren! zu

Hül - fe! zu Hül - fe! sonst bin ich ver - lo - ren!

150 Fugue No. 8.
From *Well-tempered Clavier*, Book I, BWV 853.

Johann Sebastian Bach
(1685-1750)

Minor Scales **47**

151 Gypsy melody.

Allegretto

152 Hymn. *O Gracious Father of Mankind.* Traditional Welsh melody
Words by Henry H. Tweedy (1868-1953).

O gra - cious Fa - ther of man - kind, Our spir - its' un - seen friend,

High heav - en's Lord, our hearts' dear guest, To thee our prayers as - cend.

153 Symphony No. 45, Hob. I:45, IV. Franz Joseph Haydn
(1732-1809)

Finale

Presto

154 Hymn. *Praise to the Living God.* Hebrew melody
Based on the *Yigdal* of Daniel Ben Judah fourteenth century.
Translated by Newton Mann (1836-1926) and Max Landsberg (1845-1928).

Praise to the liv - ing God! All prais - ed be his name,

Who was, and is, and is to be, And still the same!

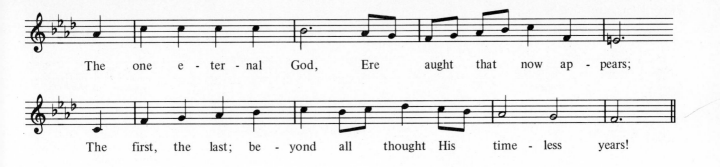

The one e-ter-nal God, Ere aught that now ap-pears;

The first, the last; be-yond all thought His time-less years!

155 Prelude, Op. 28, No. 6.

Frédéric Chopin
(1810-1849)

Lento assai

sotto voce

156 Spiritual. *Go Down, Moses.*

Ponderously

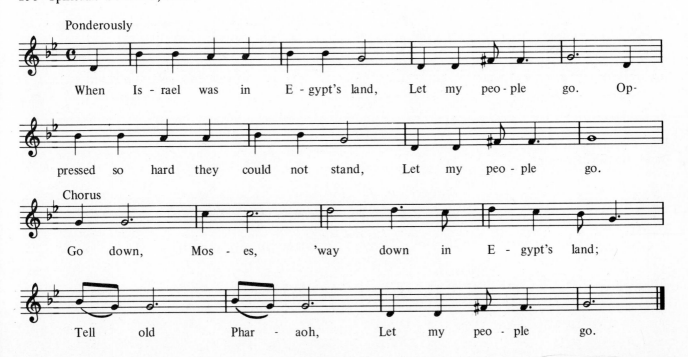

When Is - rael was in E - gypt's land, Let my peo - ple go. Op-

pressed so hard they could not stand, Let my peo - ple go.

Chorus

Go down, Mos - es, 'way down in E - gypt's land;

Tell old Phar - aoh, Let my peo - ple go.

157 Piano Sonata, Hob. XVI:36, I.

Franz Joseph Haydn
(1732-1809)

Moderato

158 Trio No. 1 for Violin, Cello, and Piano, 3rd Movement, Hob. XV.

Franz Joseph Haydn
(1732-1809)

Presto

159 *With Cunning Conniving.*

Giovanni Legrenzi
(1625-1690)

Allegretto con moto (♩.=98)

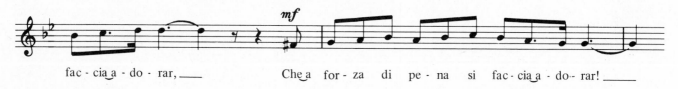

Che fie - ro cos - tu - me d'a - li - ge - ro nu - me, che a for - za di pe - na si fac - cia a - do - rar, si

fac - cia a - do - rar,___ Che a for - za di pe - na si fac - cia a - do - rar!___

160 Traditional German melody. *Jesu Meine Freude*
(*Jesus, Priceless Treasure).*

Je - sus, price - less trea - sure, Source of pur - est plea - sure,

Tru - est friend to   me.

161 Sonata.

Georg Phillip Telemann
(1681-1767)

Allegro

Violino *f*

162 *O Lord, Have Mercy.*

Alessandro Stradella
(1644-1682)

mf

se   a   te   guin - ge il   mi - o   pre - gar;

p

Non   mi   pu - ni - sca il   tu - o   ri - gor,

5 Harmony in Major Keys

163 Doxology. *Praise God from Whom All Blessings Flow.*
Words by Thomas Ken (1637-1711).

German psalter, 1551
Attr. to Louis Bourgeois
(c. 1510-c. 1561

Praise God, from whom all bless - ings flow; Praise

him, all crea - tures here be - low; Praise him a - bove, ye

heaven - ly host; Praise Fa - ther, Son, and Ho - ly Ghost.

164 *Hallelujah.*
From the oratorio *Messiah*.

George Frideric Handel
(1685-1759)

Hal - le - lu - jah! Hal - le - lu - jah! Hal - le - lu - jah! Hal - le - lu - jah!

165 **Mazurka, Op. 68, No. 3.**

Frédéric Chopin
(1810-1849)

Allegro ma non troppo

166 *Lo, How a Rose E'er Blooming.*

Michael Praetorius
(1571-1621)

Lo, how a Rose e'er bloom - ing, From ten - der___ stem ___ has sprung!

167 **Variations on an Allegretto, K 137, Anhang III,** *Tema.*

Wolfgang Amadeus Mozart
(1756-1791)

TEMA.

168 **Spiritual.** *Steal Away.*

D.C.

My Lord calls me, He calls me by the thun-der; The

trum-pet sounds with-in___ my soul, I don't have long to stay here.

169 Overture. Op. 81, *Euryanthe*.

Carl Maria Von Weber
(1786-1826)

Allegro marcato, con molto fuoco

170 Kentucky folk song. *The Riddle Song.*

I gave my love a cher-ry with-out a stone; I gave my love a chick-en with-out a bone; I

gave my love a ring__ that has no end; I gave my love a ba-by with no cry in.__

171 Chorale. *Jesus, Lead Thou On.*
From Cantata No. 57, BWV 57.

Johann Sebastian Bach
(1685-1750)

Je - sus, lead Thou on Till our rest is won;

172 *Sarrabanda.*

Johann Erasmus Kindermann
(1616-1655)

Andante commodo

173 *Joseph, O Dear Joseph Mine.*
Based on *Resonet in Laudibus.*

mf Jo - seph, O dear Jo - seph mine, Help me rock the

Child di - vine, God re - ward both thee and thine, In

par - a - dise, So prays the moth - er, Ma - ry.

174 Arietta con variazioni, Hob. XVII:2

Franz Joseph Haydn
(1732-1809)

Allegretto quasi andantino

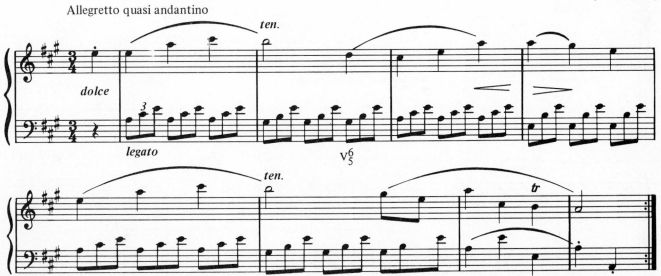

175 Menuet

Con moto

176 Sonatina, II, Andante.

Andante

Johann Sebastian Bach
(1685-1750)

V$^4_3$

178 *Ave Maria.*

Jacob Arcadelt
(c. 1505-1568)

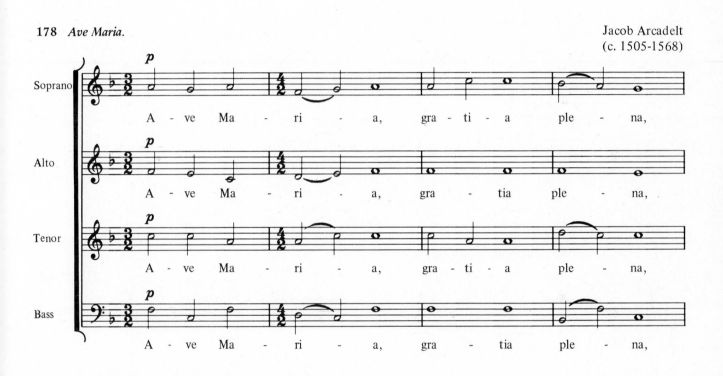

Soprano — A - ve Ma - ri - a, gra - ti - a ple - na,

Alto — A - ve Ma - ri - a, gra - tia ple - na,

Tenor — A - ve Ma - ri - a, gra - ti - a ple - na,

Bass — A - ve Ma - ri - a, gra - tia ple - na,

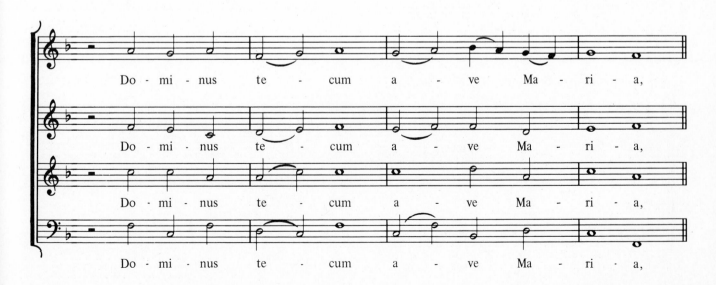

Do - mi - nus te - cum a - ve Ma - ri - a,

Do - mi - nus te - cum a - ve Ma - ri - a,

Do - mi - nus te - cum a - ve Ma - ri - a,

Do - mi - nus te - cum a - ve Ma - ri - a,

6 Harmony in Minor Keys

179 *Album for the Young,* Op. 68, No. 8.

Robert Schumann
(1810-1856)

180 Traditional American song. *The Erie Canal.*

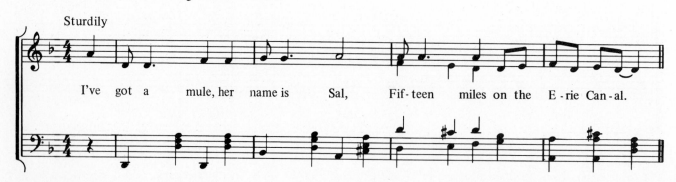

I've got a mule, her name is Sal, Fif-teen miles on the E-rie Can-al.

181 **Russian folk song.** *Song of the Volga Boatmen.*

Heavily

Yo heave ho! Yo heave ho!

Once more pull to the shore, Yo heave ho!

182 *Adoramus Te.*

Giovanni Pierluigi Palestrina
(1525-1594)

Soprano: A - do - ra - mus - te Chri - ste

Alto: A - do - ra - mus - te Chri - ste

Tenor: A - do - ra - mus - te Chri - ste

Bass: A - do - ra - mus - te Chri - ste

183 **Hymn.** *O Gracious Father of Mankind.*
Words by Henry H. Tweedy (1868-1953).

Traditional Welsh melody,
Hymnau a Thonau, 1865

O gra - cious Fa - ther of man - kind, Our spir - its' un - seen friend,

ii6
5

Harmony in Minor Keys **61**

184 *Et in Terra Pax Hominibus.*
From *Gloria*, No. 2.

Antonio Vivaldi
(1675-1741)

185 American folk song. *Willie the Weeper.*

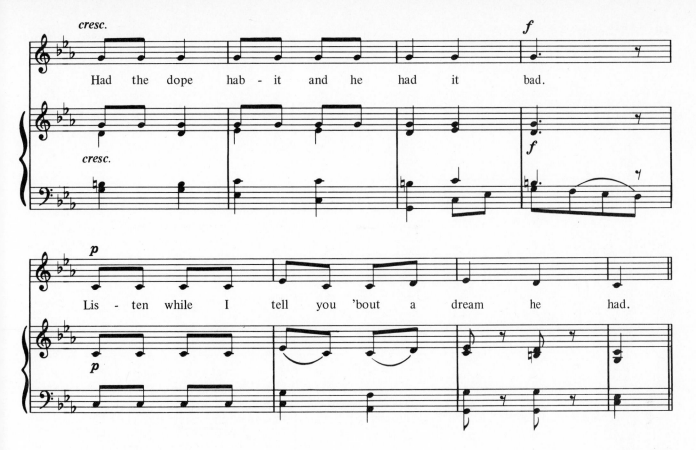

Had the dope hab-it and he had it bad.

Lis-ten while I tell you 'bout a dream he had.

186 *Le menaccie i fieri accenti.*
From the opera *La Forza del Destino,* Act IV.

Guiseppe Verdi
(1813-1901)

Andante

Le me - nac - cie‿i fie - ri‿ac - cen ti, por - tin se - co‿in pre - da‿i

ven - ti, per - do - na - te - mi pie - tà, O fra - tel, pie - tà, pie - tà.

V7

187 Offertorium.

From *Requiem Mass,* K 626.

Wolfgang Amadeus Mozart
(1756-1791)

188 Spiritual. *Sometimes I Feel Like a Motherless Child.*

Sadly

Some-times I feel like a moth-er-less child, Some-times I feel like a

moth-er-less child, Some-times I feel like a moth-er-less child, _____ A

long way _ from home, _____ A long way _ from home.

189 *But Who May Abide.*
From the oratorio *Messiah.*

George Frideric Handel
(1685-1759)

Larghetto (♩=88)

Bass

But who may a - bide the day of His com - ing?

190 Sixteenth century English carol.
Lullay, Thou Little Tiny Child.
Coventry carol. Words by Robert Croo.

Lul-lay, Thou lit - tle ti - ny Child, By, by, lul-ly, lul - lay; _____ Lul - lay, Thou lit - tle

ti - ny Child, By, by, lul - ly, lul - lay. _____

191 Chorale. *Our Father, Thou in Heav'n Above,* BWV 416.

Johann Sebastian Bach
(1685-1750)

Our Fa - ther, Thou in heav'n a - bove, Who bid - dest us to

dwell in love, As breth - ren of one fam - i - ly,

192 *Wherefore Do the Heathen Clamor?*
From *Christmas Oratorio.*

Camille Saint-Saëns
(1835-1921)

Georg Philipp Telemann
(1681-1767)

7 Dominant Seventh Chords

194 *Album for the Young*, Op. 68, *Soldiers' March.*

Robert Schumann
(1810-1856)

195 Waltz.

Franz Schubert
(1797-1828)

196 Hymn. *All Hail the Power of Jesus' Name.*

Words by Edward Perronet (1726-1792). Altered by
John Rippon (1751-1836).

James Ellor
(1819-1899)

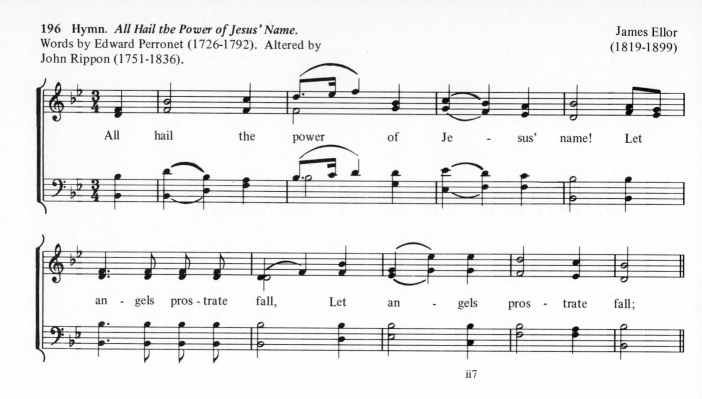

All hail the power of Je - sus' name! Let

an - gels pros - trate fall, Let an - gels pros - trate fall;

ii7

197 American game song. *The Finger Band.*

Playfully

The fin - ger band has come to town, the fin - ger band has

come to town, the fin - ger band has come to town so

ear - ly in ___ the morn - ing.

198 *Jingle Bells.*

James Pierpont
(1822-1893)

Joyously

Dash - ing through the snow in a one horse o - pen sleigh, O'er the fields we go,

laugh-ing all the way; ___ Bells on bob-tails ring, mak - ing spir - its bright,

Oh, what fun it is to sing a sleigh - ing song to night.

Frédéric Chopin
(1810-1849)

Vivace

200 *The Blue Tail Fly (Jimmy Crack Corn).*

Dan Emmett
(1815-1904)

Boldly

Chorus

Jim-my crack corn   and   I don't care,   Jim-my crack corn   and   I don't care,

rit.   a tempo

Jim - my crack corn   and   I don't care,   my mas - ter's gone a - way.

V_2^4/IV

201 Carol. *We Three Kings of Orient Are.*
Words from Matthew 2:1-11. Edited by
John H. Hopkins, Jr.

John H. Hopkins, Jr.
(1820-1891)

We three Kings of O - ri - ent are; Bear - ing

gifts, we trav - erse a - far, Field and foun - tain,

G:

moor and moun - tain, Fol - low - ing yon - der star.

e:

202 Sonata, Aria (II).

Carl Heinrich Graun
(1704-1759)

203 Christmas song. *Up on the Housetop.*
Words by Benjamin R. Handby.

Benjamin R. Handby
(1833-1867)

Up on the house-top ___ rein-deer pause, Out jumps good old ___

San-ta Claus; ___ Down thro' the chim-ney with lots of toys,

All for the lit-tle ones ___ Christ-mas joys.

206 *I Love Paris.*
From the musical *Can-Can.* Words by Cole Porter.

Cole Porter
(1892-1964)

Refrain

Slow Fox-trot tempo

I love Par · is in the spring-time. ___

p legato

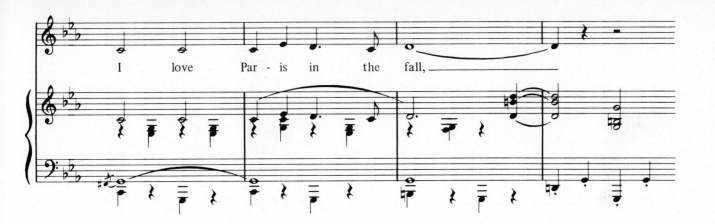

I love Par - is in the fall, _____

205 English folk song. *Charlie Is My Darling.*

Char - lie is my dar - ling, my dar - ling, my dar - ling,

Char - lie is my dar - ling the young chev - a - lier. _____

206 Christmas carol. *Deck the Halls.*

Old Welsh tune

Deck the halls with boughs of hol - ly, Fa, la, la, la, la, la, la, la, la.

207 Hymn. *I Am Thine, O Lord.*
From Hebrews 10:22. Edited by Fanny J. Crosby
(1820-1915).

William H. Doane
(1832-1915)

208 Hymn. *When I Survey the Wondrous Cross.*
From Galatians 6:14. Edited by Isaac Watts (1674-1748).

Ancient chant,
harmony by Lowell Mason
(1792-1872).

And pour con - tempt on all my pride.

ii$^6_5$

209 Mass. K 258, *Gloria.*

Wolfgang Amadeus Mozart
(1756-1791)

Soprano: Glo - ri - a, glo - ri - a in ex - cel - sis De - o

Alto: Glo - ri - a, glo - ri - a in ex - cel - sis De - o

Tenor: Glo - ri - a, glo - ri - a in ex - cel - sis De - o

Bass: Glo - ri - a, glo - ri - a in ex - cel - sis De - o

et in ter - ra pax ho - mi - ni - bus bo - nae vo - lun - ta - tis;

et in ter - ra pax, pax ho - mi - ni - bus bo - nae vo - lun - ta - tis;

et in ter - ra pax ho - mi - ni - bus bo - nae vo - lun - ta - tis;

et in ter - ra pax ho - mi - ni - bus bo - nae bo - nae vo - lun - ta - tis;

Dominant Seventh Chords 77

210 Hymn. *For the Beauty of the Earth.*
Words by Folliot S. Pierpont (1835-1917).

Harmony by W. H. Monk
(1823-1889)

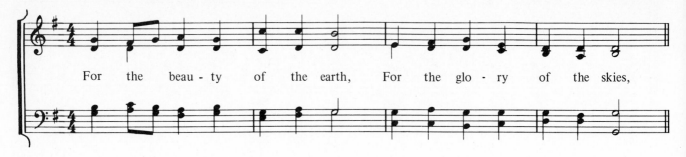

For   the   beau - ty   of   the   earth,   For   the   glo - ry   of   the   skies,

211 Piano Sonata, K 545, I.

Wolfgang Amadeus Mozart
(1756-1791)

Allegro

212 *The Heavens Are Telling.*
From the oratorio *The Creation,* No. 13, Hob. XXI:2.

Franz Joseph Haydn
(1732-1809)

Allegro

Chorus

Soprano — Die Him - mel   er - zäh - len die   Eh - re   Got - tes.

Alto — The   hea - vens   are   tel - ling the   glo - ry   of   God.

Tenor — Die Him - mel   er - zäh - len die   Eh - re   Got - tes.

Bass — The   hea - vens   are   tel - ling the   glo - ry   of   God.

Allegro

213 *Lift Thine Eyes to the Mountains.*
From the oratorio *Elijah,* No. 28, Trio.

Felix Mendelssohn
(1809-1847)

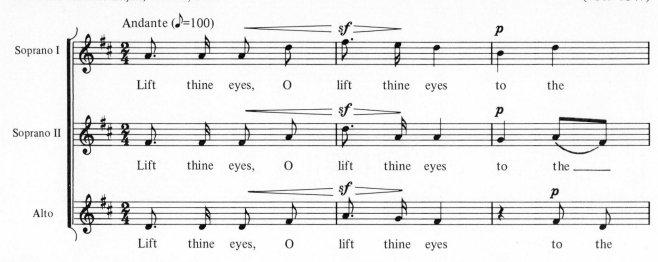

Soprano I

Lift   thine   eyes,   O   lift   thine   eyes   to   the

Soprano II

Lift   thine   eyes,   O   lift   thine   eyes   to   the ____

Alto

Lift   thine   eyes,   O   lift   thine   eyes   to   the

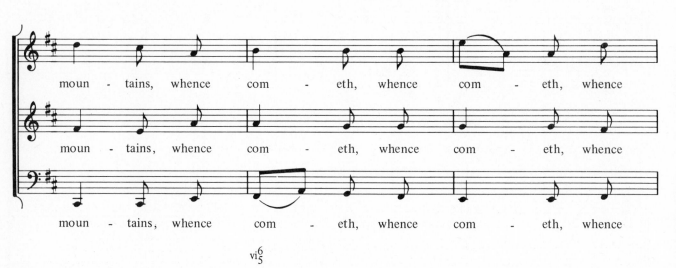

moun - tains,   whence   com - eth,   whence   com - eth,   whence

moun - tains,   whence   com - eth,   whence   com - eth,   whence

moun - tains,   whence   com - eth,   whence   com - eth,   whence

vi⁶₅

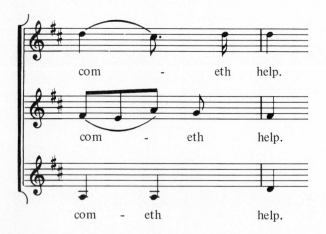

com - eth   help.

com - eth   help.

com - eth   help.

8 Phrase Structures and Cadences

214 Scottish folk song. *Bluebells of Scotland.*

Oh, where tell me where is your ___ High - land lad - die gone.

215 Hymn. *O Young Divine and Golden.*   John B. Dykes
Words by John S. B. Monsell (1811-1875).   (1823-1876)

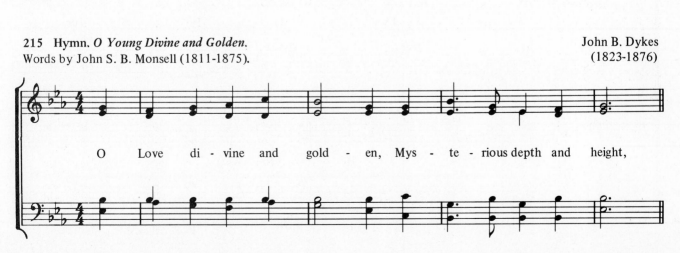

O   Love di - vine and gold - en, Mys - te - rious depth and height,

216 Traditional Scottish melody. *Loch Lomond.*

By __ yon bon-nie banks, And by __ yon bon-nie braes, Where the sun shines bright on Loch Lo - mon,

217 *Lift Up Your Heads.*
From the oratorio, *Messiah*.

George Frideric Handel
(1685-1759)

A tempo ordinario (♩ =76)

Soprano: the Lord of Hosts, the Lord of

Alto: the Lord of Hosts, the Lord of Hosts, _____

Tenor: the Lord of Hosts, the Lord of

Bass: the Lord of Hosts, the Lord of

Hosts, the Lord of Hosts, He is the King _____

_____ the Lord of Hosts, He is the King, _____ the King of

Hosts, the Lord of Hosts, He is the King of glo - ry, the

Hosts, the Lord of Hosts, He is the King of

Johannes Brahms
(1833-1897)

219 *Agnus Dei.*
From Missa Brevis, *Sancti Joannis Deo,* Hob. XXII:7.

Franz Joseph Haydn
(1732-1809)

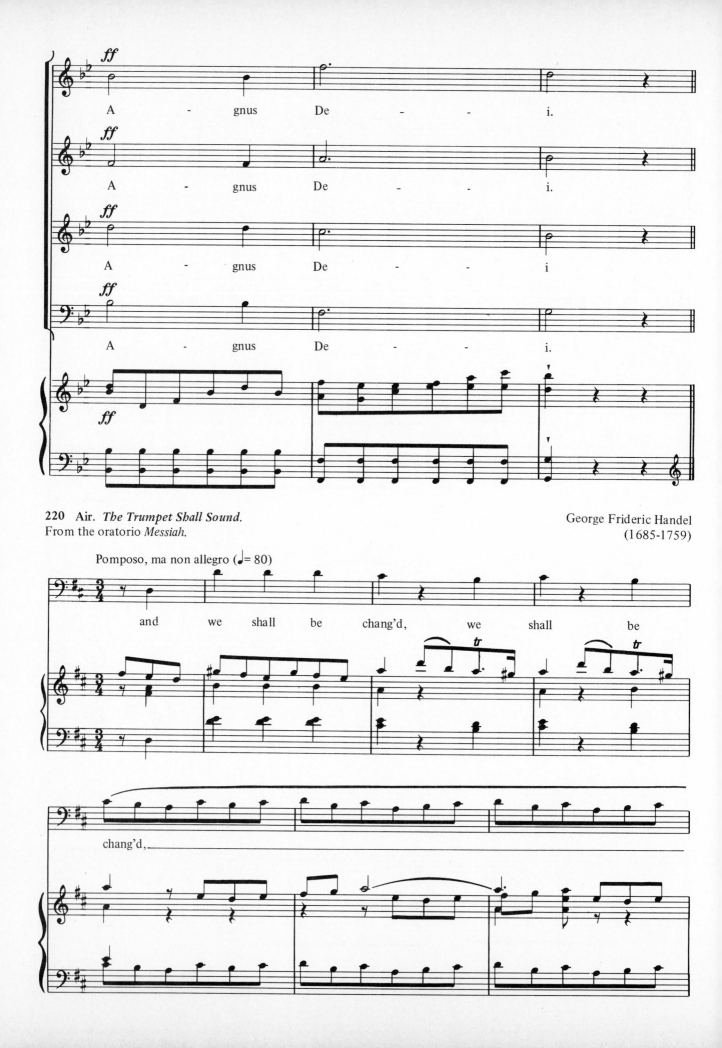

220 Air. *The Trumpet Shall Sound.*
From the oratorio *Messiah.*

George Frideric Handel
(1685-1759)

Pomposo, ma non allegro (♩ = 80)

and

Adagio

we shall be chang'd, we shall be chang'd.

221 American game song. *Bow Belinda.*

Dancelike

Bow, bow, bow Be - lin - da; Bow, bow, bow Be - lin - da;

Bow, bow, bow, Be - lin - da; Won't you be my dar - ling?

From the opera *Magic Flute*, K 620, Act I, No. 5.

Wolfgang Amadeus Mozart
(1756-1791)

224 **Piano Sonata No. 35, Hob. XVI:35, III.**   Franz Joseph Haydn
(1732-1809)

225 Song from the British Isles. *The Girl I Left Behind Me.*

Lively

I'm_ lone-some since I crossed the hill and o'er the moor_and_val - ley, Such_

heav - y thoughts my heart do fill since part - ing with my_ Sal - ly.

226 Spiritual. *Swing Low, Sweet Chariot.*

Soprano

Swing low, sweet char - i - ot_ com-in' for to car - ry me

Alto

Swing low, sweet char - i - ot_ com-in' for to car - ry me

Tenor

Swing low, char - i - ot com-in' for to car - ry me

Bass

Swing low, char - i - ot com-in' for to car - ry me

home, Swing low, sweet char - i - ot

home, Swing low, sweet char - i - ot

home, Swing low, char - i - ot

home, Swing low, char - i - ot

com - in' for to car - ry me home.

com - in' for to car - ry me home.

com - in' home.

com - in' home.

227 **Mother Goose rhyme.** *Jack and Jill.*

Playfully

Jack and Jill went up the hill to fetch a pail of

wa - ter; Jack fell down and broke his crown, and

rit.

Jill came tum - bling af - ter.

228 French carol. *Sing We Noel.*

Sing we the sto - ry of the Sav - iour's ___ birth!

Peace and good - will to all ___ on earth!

ii7

229 Minuet.

Ludwig van Beethoven
(1770-1827)

230 Traditional Scottish song. *Auld Lang Syne.*

Should auld ac-quain-tance be for-got, And__ nev - er brought to mind? Should

auld ac-quain-tance be for-got, And__ days of auld lang syne?

232 American folk song. *Wagoner's Lad.*

9 Form

Section A

BINARY AND ROUNDED BINARY

233   Symphony No. 94, *Surprise*, Hob. I:94, II.

Franz Joseph Haydn
(1732-1809)

Andante

234 Minuet.

Anonymous

From the *Notebook for Anna Magdalena Bach* (1725).

Wolfgang Amadeus Mozart
(1756-1791)

236 *Little Dance in F.*

Franz Joseph Haydn
(1739-1809)

237 Piano Sonata, K 284, III, *Theme with Variations.*

Wolfgang Amadeus Mozart
(1756-1791)

238 Viennese Sonatina, *Sonatine IV*, Andante grazioso.

Wolfgang Amadeus Mozart
(1756-1791)

Section B

SIMPLE AND COMPOUND TERNARY

239 Mazurka No. 43, Op. Posthumous 67, No. 2.

Frédéric Chopin
(1810-1849)

240 Song cycle. *Die Schöne Müllerin,* Op. 25, No. 19, *The Miller and the Brook.*

Franz Schubert
(1797-1828)

Mässig (Moderato) (Der Müller.) (The Miller)

Wo ein treu-es Her-ze in Lie-be ver-

geht, da wel-ken die Li-lien auf je-dem

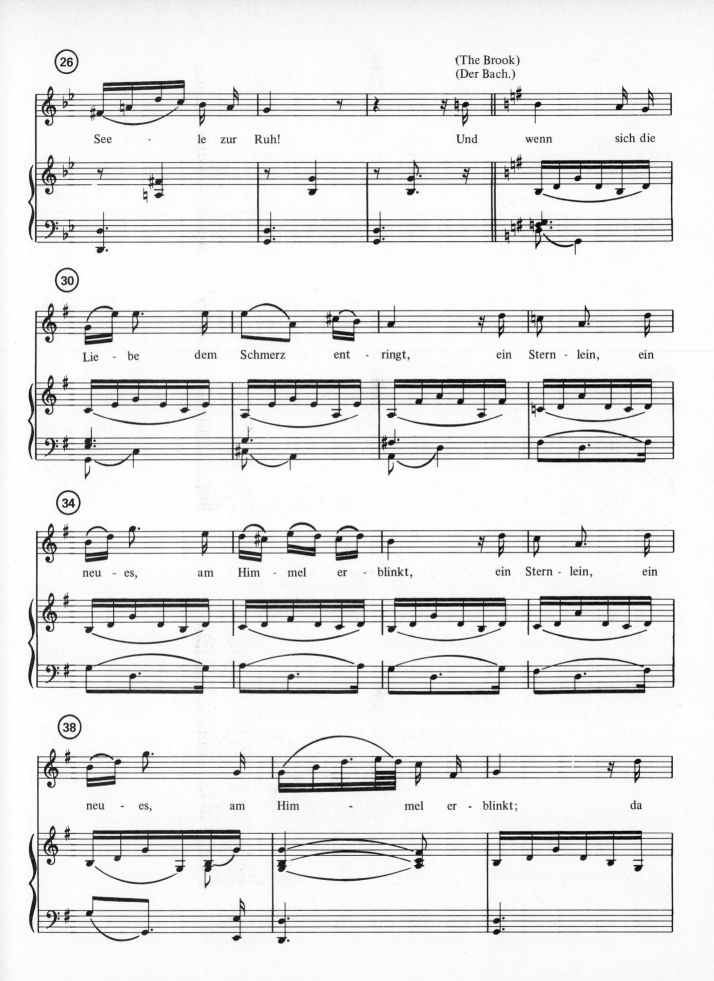

(The Brook)
(Der Bach.)

See - le zur Ruh! Und wenn sich die

Lie - be dem Schmerz ent - ringt, ein Stern - lein, ein

neu - es, am Him - mel er - blinkt, ein Stern - lein, ein

neu - es, am Him - mel er - blinkt; da

Form 107

gehn al - le Mor - gen zur Er - de her - ab.

(Der Müller.) (The Miller)

Ach Bäch - lein, lie - bes Bäch - lein, du meinst es so

gut; ach Bäch - lein, a - ber weißt du, wie

Lie - - be tut? _____ Ach

un - ten, da un - ten die küh - le Ruh! _____ ach

Bäch - lein, lie - bes Bäch - lein, so sin - ge nur zu, ach

Bäch - lein, lie - bes Bäch - lein, so sin - ge nur zu.

Franz Joseph Haydn
(1732-1809)

Menuetto.

Allegretto.

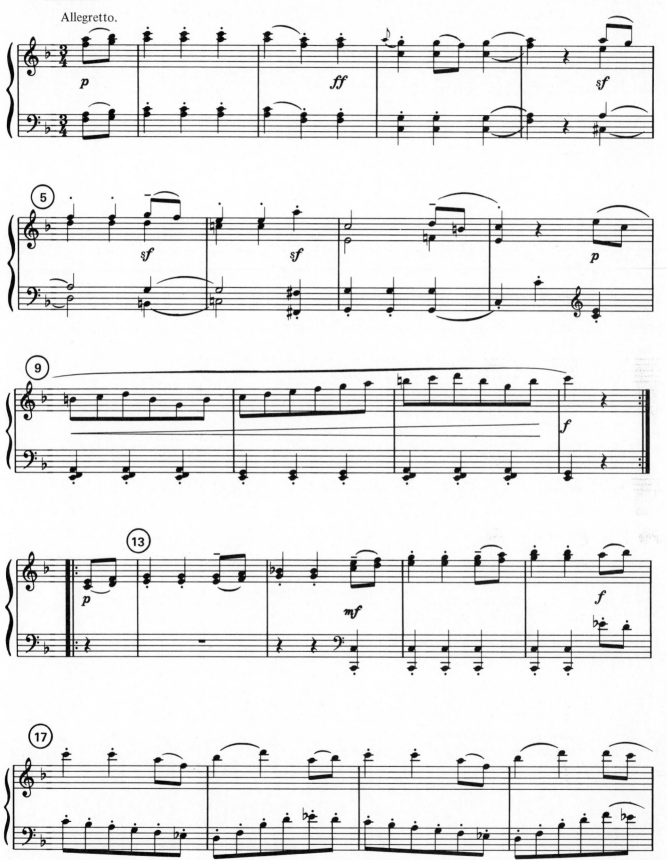

Fine

Menuetto d.c.

242 Piano Sonata, K 282, II.

Wolfgang Amadeus Mozart
(1756-1791)

Menuetto I.

Men. I. da Capo.

Section C

RONDO

243 Piano Sonata, Hob. XVI:37, III.

Franz Joseph Haydn
(1732-1809)

Finale

Presto, ma non troppo

Section D

SONATA — ALLEGRO

244 Piano Sonata, K 309, I.

Wolfgang Amadeus Mozart
(1756-1791)

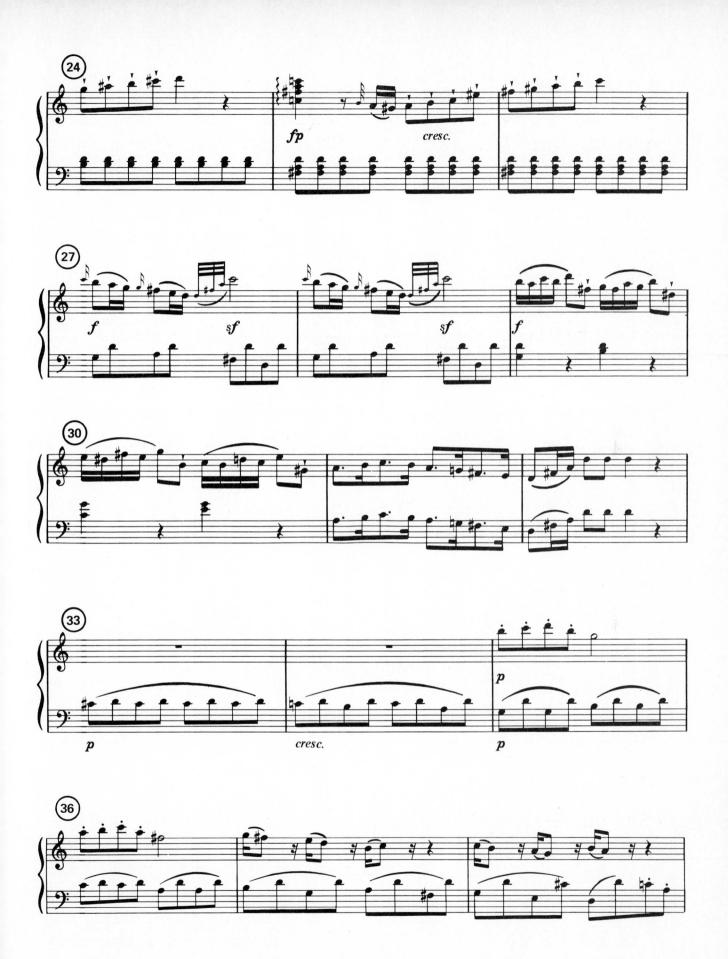

245   Serenade. *Eine Kleine Nachtmusik*, K 525, I.

Wolfgang Amadeus Mozart
(1756-1791)

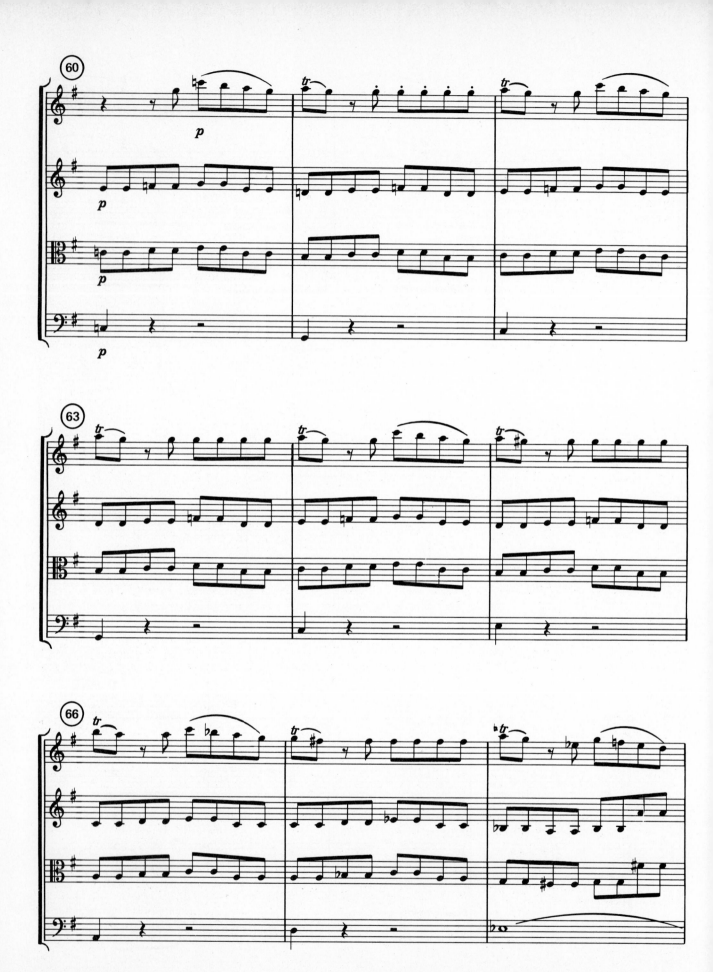

Section E

CONTRAPUNTAL FORMS

246 Two-Part Invention, No. 1, BWV 772.

Johann Sebastian Bach.
(1685-1750)

247 Fugue XVI.
From *Well-Tempered Clavier*, Book I, BWV 861.

Johann Sebastian Bach
(1685-1750)

248 *And the Glory of the Lord.*
From the oratorio *Messiah*.

George Frideric Handel
(1685-1759)

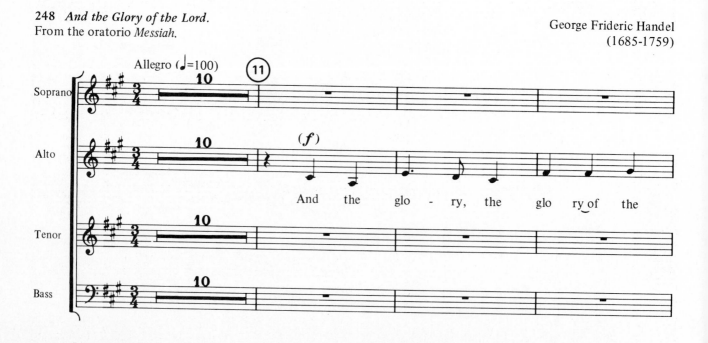

And the glo - ry, the glo ry of the

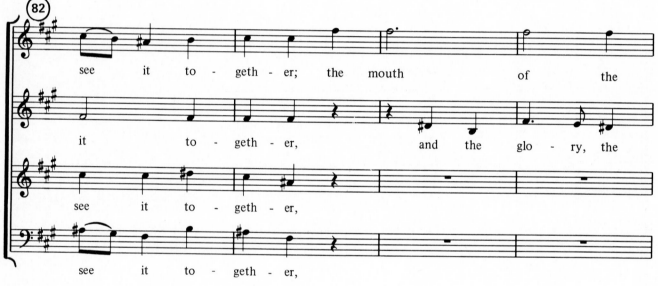

RHYTHMIC READING

1 Simple Meters

$\frac{2}{4}$ $\frac{3}{4}$ $\frac{4}{4}$ WITH NO BEAT DIVISION

1

Andante

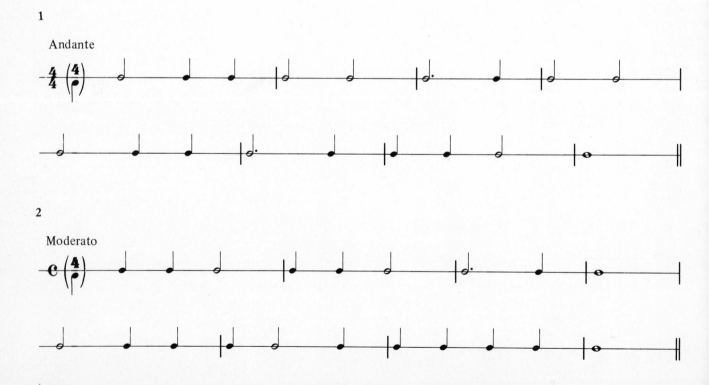

2

Moderato

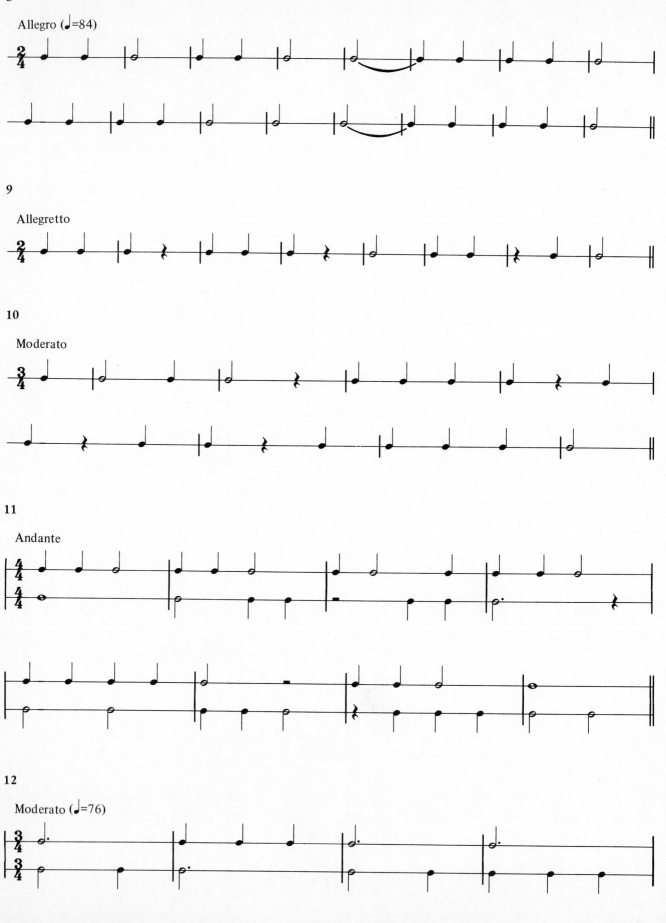

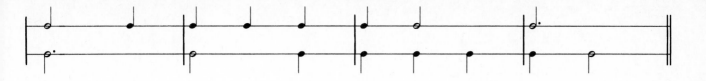

13

Allegretto

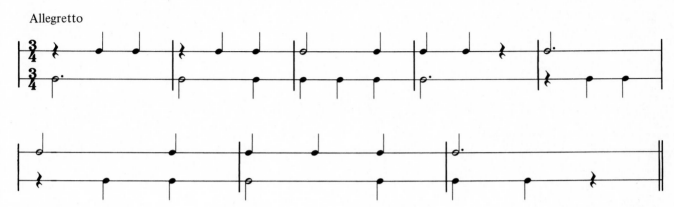

14

Andantino

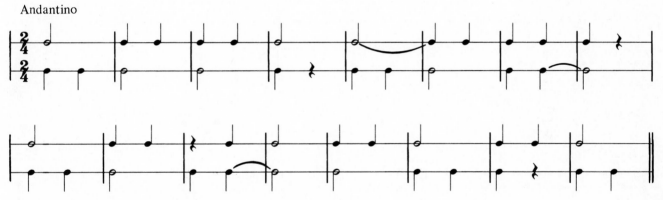

15

Larghetto

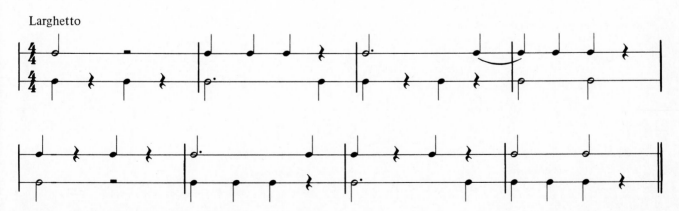

2/4　　**3/4**　　**4/4**　WITH　♪　　♩.

16

Moderato

17

Allegro

18

Andante

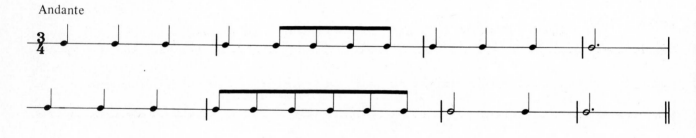

19

Adagio (♩=56)

20

Allegro

21

Moderato

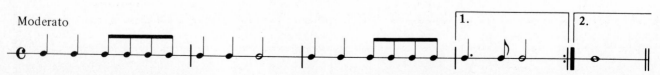

27

28

29

30

Section C

2/4   3/4   4/4 WITH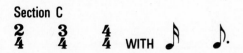

31

Moderato

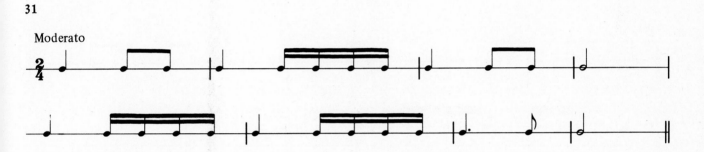

32

Moderato (♩=84)

33

Vivace

34

Andantino

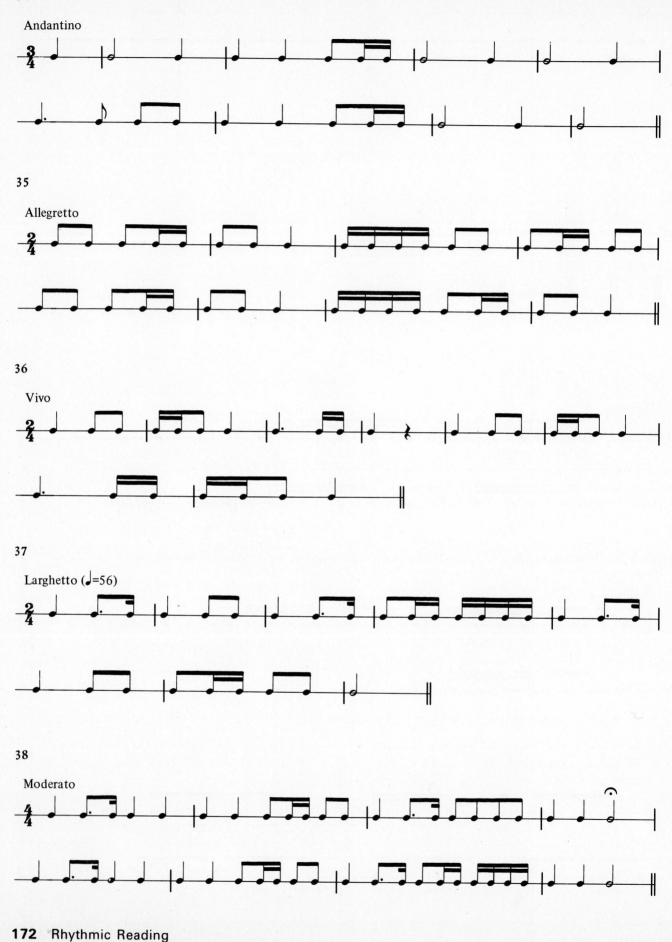

35

Allegretto

36

Vivo

37

Larghetto (♩=56)

38

Moderato

Section D
OTHER SIMPLE METERS $\frac{2}{2}$ $\frac{3}{2}$ $\frac{4}{2}$ ¢ $\frac{3}{8}$

46

Adagio

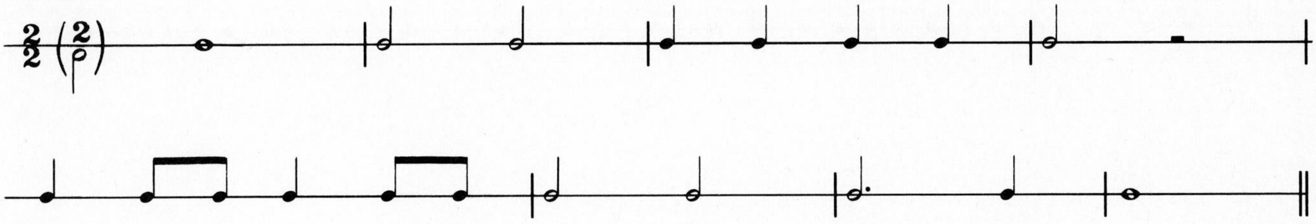

47

Larghetto (♩=50)

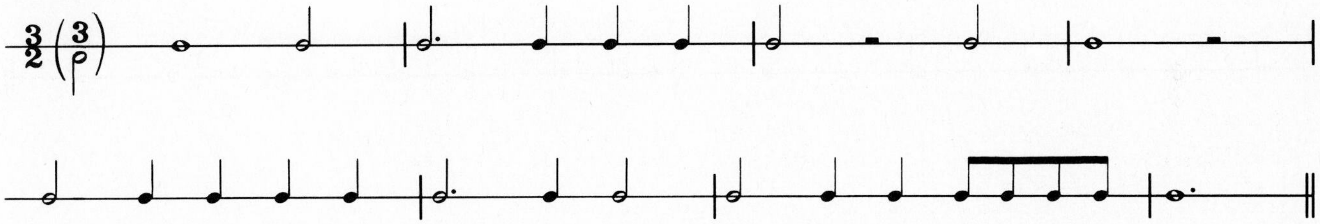

48

Andantino

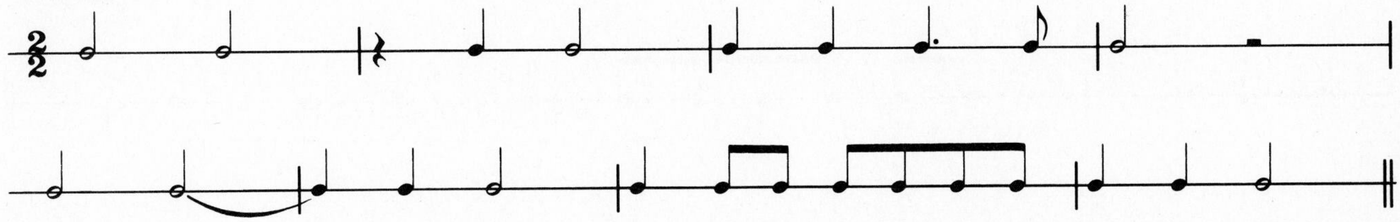

49

Andante

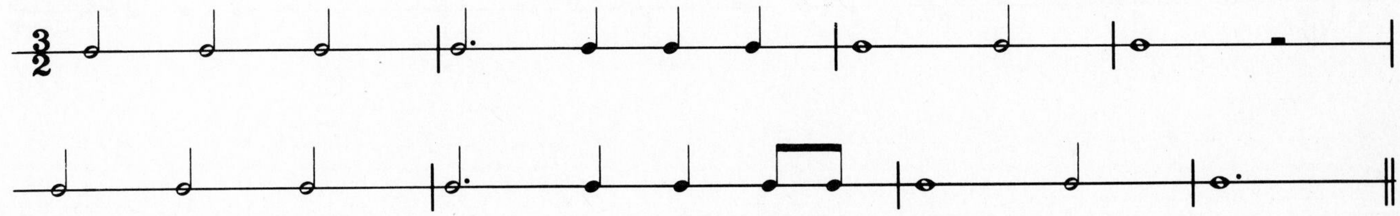

50

Lento

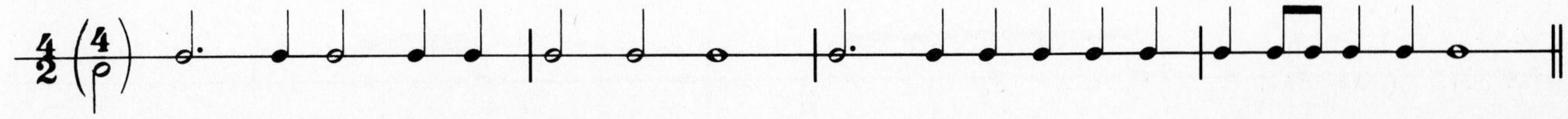

56

Andante

57

Larghetto

58

Moderato

59

Moderato (♩=80)

60

Andantino

2 Compound Meters

6 9 12
8 8 8   WITH NO BEAT DIVISION

61

Andante

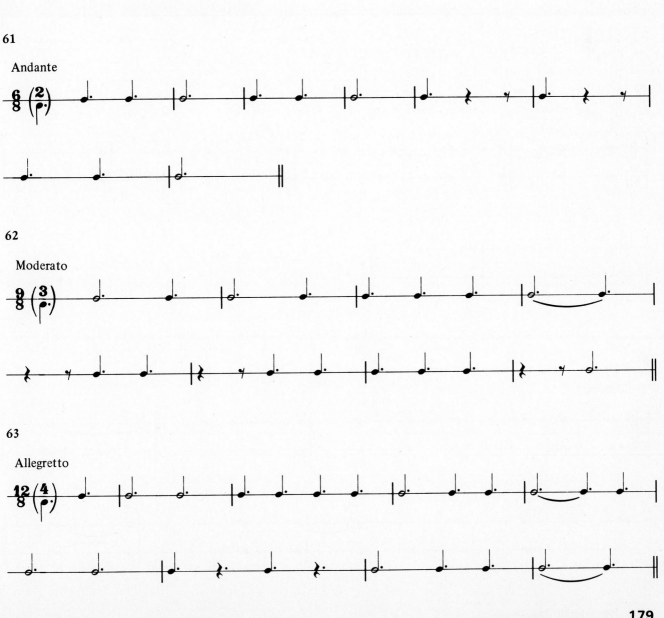

62

Moderato

63

Allegretto

68

Lento

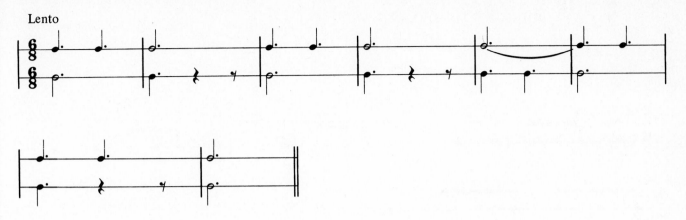

69

Moderato

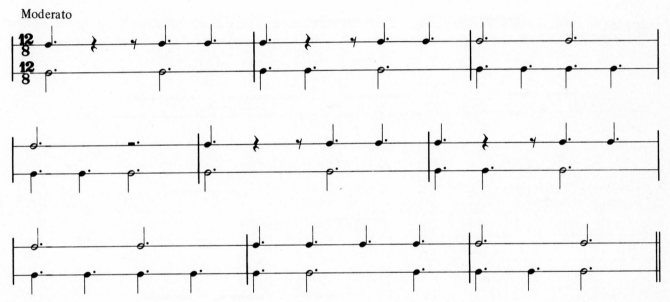

70

Allegretto

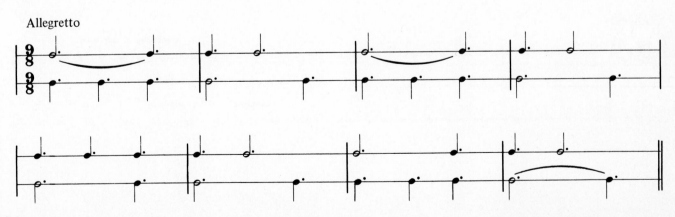

Section B

$\frac{6}{8}$ $\frac{9}{8}$ $\frac{12}{8}$ WITH ♪ ♩

71

Presto

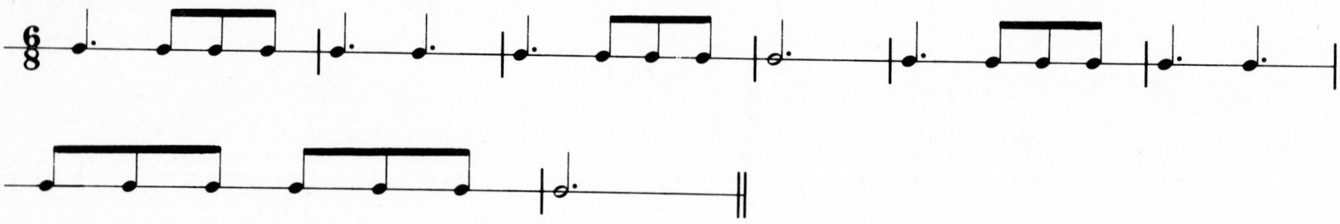

72

Vivace

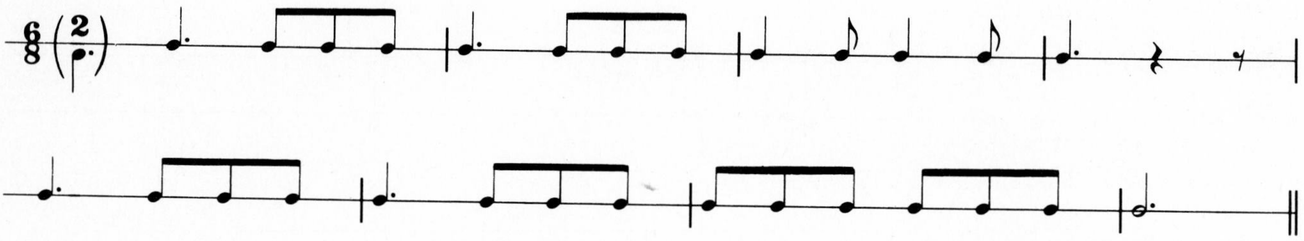

73

Moderato

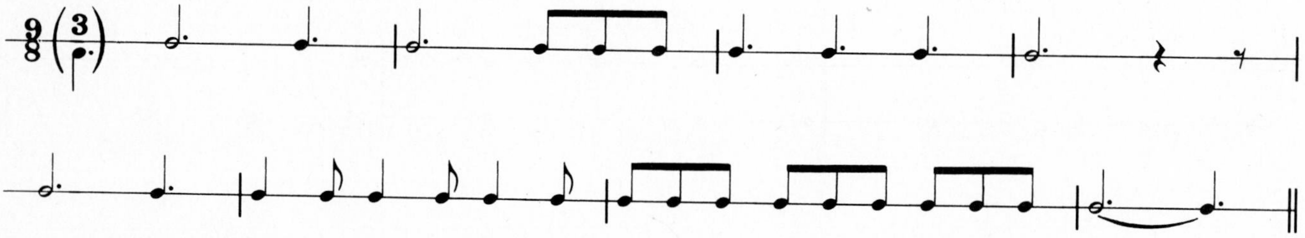

74

Andante

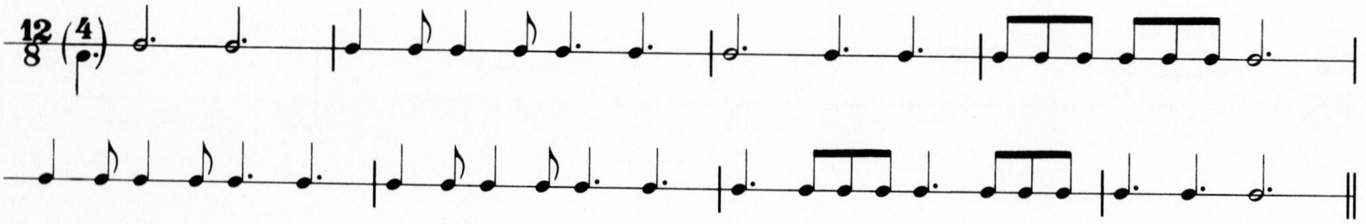

75

Andante (♩. =74)

76

Moderato

77

Allegretto

78

Allegretto

79

Lento

80

Allegro

81

Schnell

82

Mässig

83

Etwas bewegt (♩.=110)

84

Allegro

85

Bewegt (♩.=124)

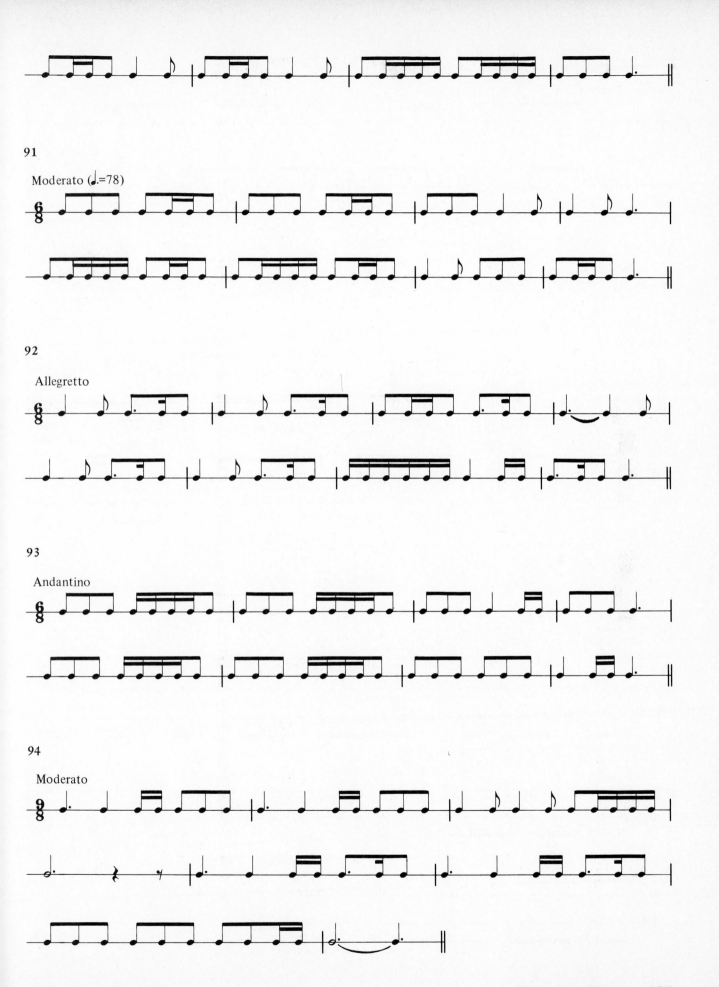

95

Vivace (♩=112)

96

Très moderé

97

Anime

98

Vif

99

Vivace

100

Allegretto

PART III

SIGHT SINGING

1 Major Keys with Seconds

7

Moderato

8

Piacevole

9

Allegretto

10

Giocoso

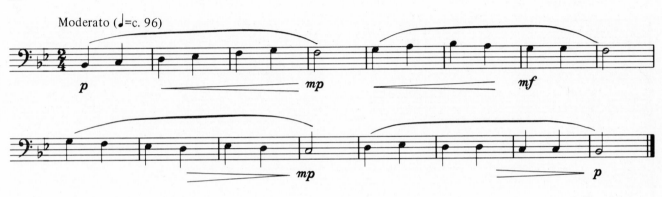

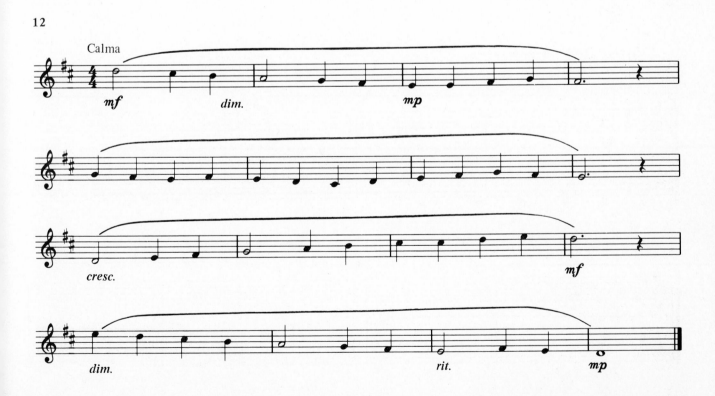

13

14

15

16

Allegretto

17

Allegro innocente

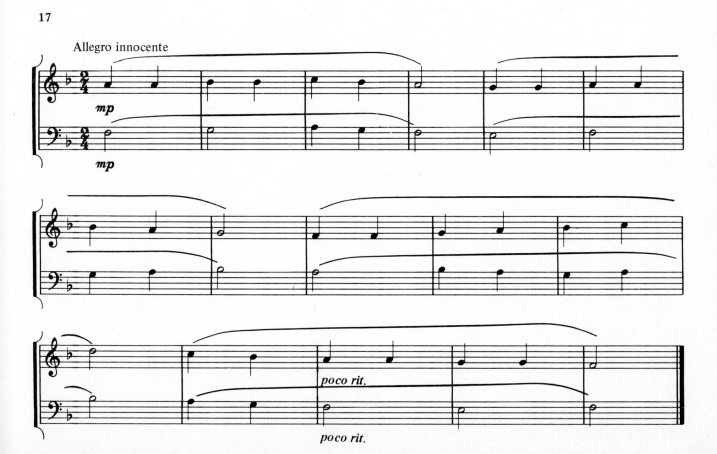

2 Minor Keys with Seconds

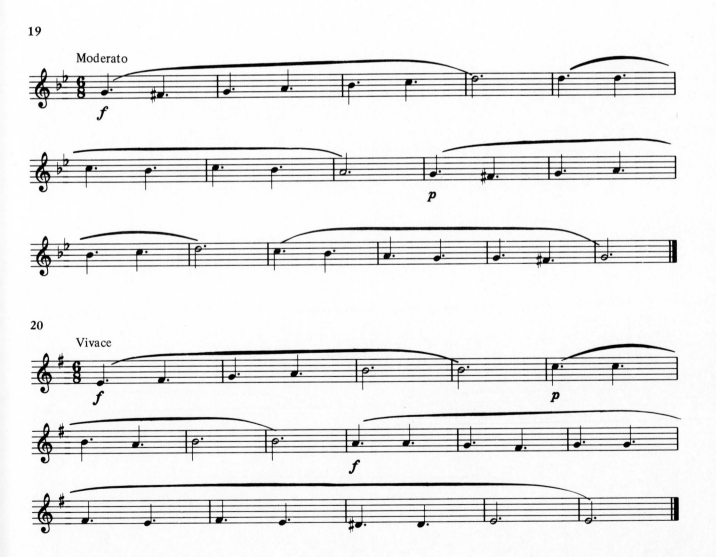

21

22

23

24

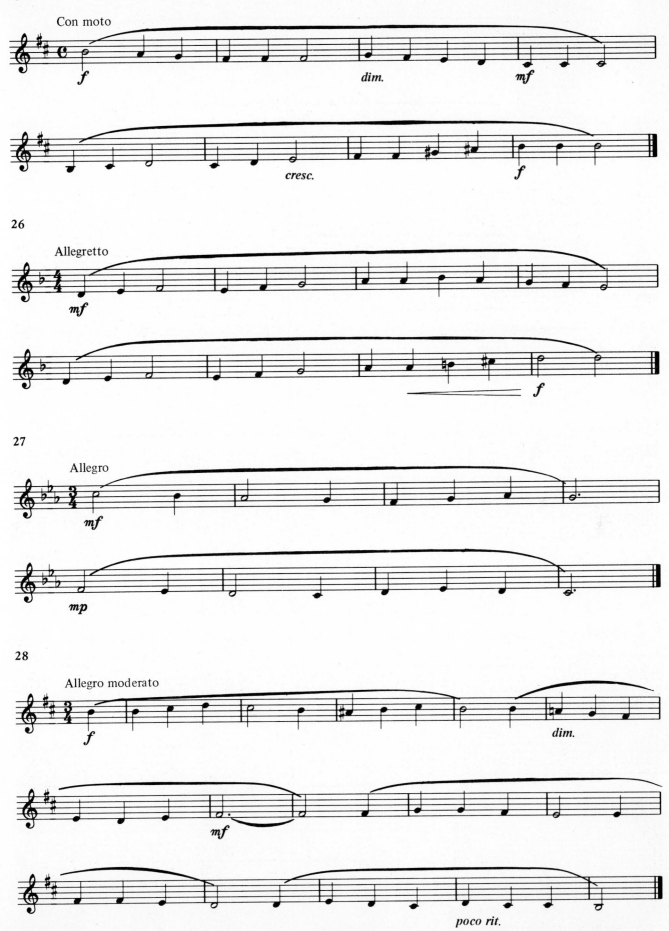

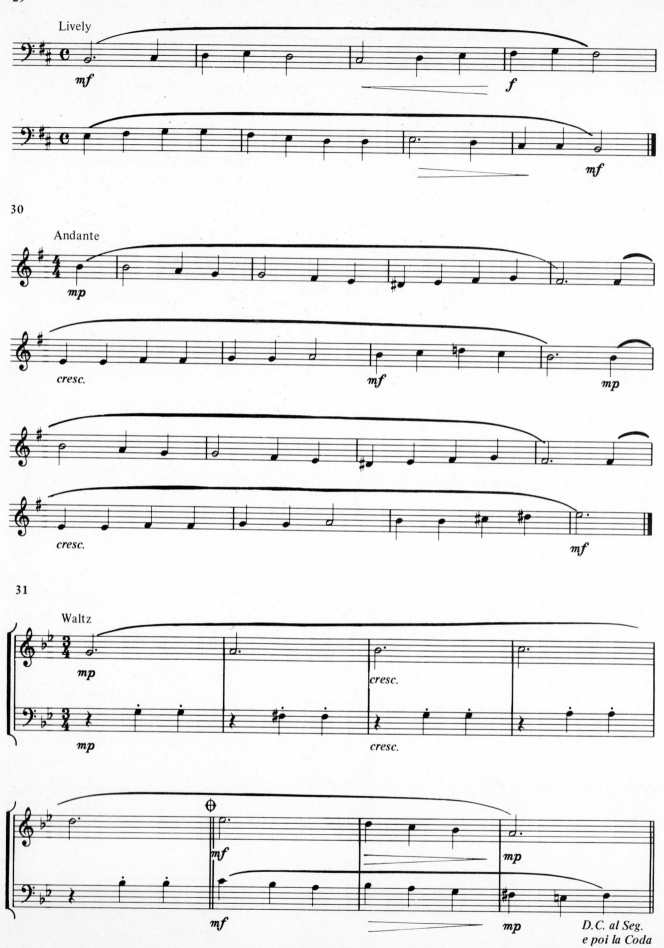

29

Lively

30

Andante

31

Waltz

D.C. al Seg.
e poi la Coda

32

33

34

35

36

3 Major and Minor Thirds

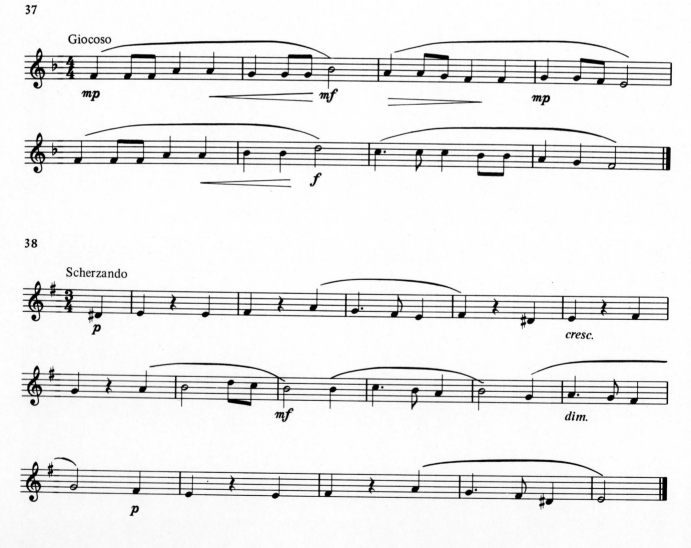

39

40

41

42

53

55

56

Glossary

ADAGIETTO (ah dah ji ET oh). A slow tempo but not as slow as adagio; a short adagio composition or movement.

ADAGIO (ah DAH jio). A slow tempo; a composition or movement written in a slow tempo.

AFFETUOSO (ah fet too OH zoh). To be performed with "feeling" or "affection."

ALLANT (ahl lahnh). *En allant*, moving, flowing.

ALLEGRETTO (ahl lay GRET toh). A lively tempo but not as fast as allegro; a short allegro movement.

ALLEGRO (ahl LAY groh). A rather fast tempo; a composition or movement written in a fast tempo.

ANDANTE (ahn DAHN tay). A rather slow tempo; a composition or movement in a slow tempo.

ANDANTINO (ahn dahn TEE noh). Currently used to indicate a tempo somewhat faster than *andante*; during the Classic period the term indicated a tempo somewhat slower than *andante*.

ANIMÉ (ah nee MAY). Lively, animated.

ARIETTA (ah ree EH tah). A "little" aria; a selection that is shorter and less elaborate than an aria (solo song).

ASSAI (ah SAH ee). Very. *Allegro assai*, very fast.

BALLADE (bah LAHD). A lyric instrumental piece.

BALLANDO (bah LAHN do). Dancing.

BEWEGT (be VAYGT). With motion.

BINARY. A two-part form used for an entire composition or for sections of a larger form.

BREVIS (BRAY vees). Short.

BRIO (BREE oh). Spirited. *Con brio*, with spirit.

BWV. An abbreviation for *Bach Werke-Verzeichnis* (*Index to Bach's Works*) compiled by Wolfgang Schmieder. All numbers correspond to the listings in this catalog.

CALMA (KAHL mah). Calm.

CANTABILE (kahn TAH bee lay). To be performed in a smooth, flowing style; in a "singing" fashion.

CANTATA (kahn TAH tah). Generally a composition for chorus, vocal soloists, and instrumental accompaniment.

CHORALE (kor AHL). The melodies to which hymns are sung in the Protestant church.

CLAVIER (klah VEER). A French word meaning "keyboard."

CODA (KOH dah). A concluding section which is added to the proper form of a composition or movement.

COMODO (KOH moh doh). To be performed at a leisurely pace.

COMPOUND TERNARY. A three-part form used for the structure of a composition or movement of a work. Each section, A – B – A, subdivides into a binary or rounded binary form.

CON (kohn). With.

CONCERTO (kon CHAIR toh). A composition written for a solo instrument and orchestral accompaniment. It is usually in three movements: fast, slow, fast.

COUNTERPOINT. A technique of composition which combines two or more distinct melodies into a single musical fabric.

CRESCENDO (kreh SHEN doh). An indication for a gradual increase in volume.

CYCLE. The term used for a group of compositions which are related in some way, such as in text or topic; very often a group of songs, but could also be found in instrumental music.

DECRESCENDO (dee kray SHEN doh). A dynamic indication for a gradual decrease in intensity.

DIMINUENDO (dee mee noo EN doh). An indication for a gradual decrease in volume.

DOLCE (DOHL chay). An indication for a soft, sweet, and rather sentimental interpretation.

EN (ahn). In.

ENERGICO (ay NAIR jee koh). Energetic.

FORTE (FOHR tay). A dynamic indication meaning to play or sing loudly. The abbreviation is *f*.

FUGUE (fewg). A contrapuntal (written in counterpoint) composition in two or more parts. The *subject*, musical theme, is stated alone by a single part at the beginning and imitated by separate entries of the remaining parts. The precise number of components varies, but all fugues are based on sections which announce and imitate the subject, alternating with episodes — sections which develop the subject.

FUOCO (foo OH koh). To be performed in a lively and flashy manner.

GIGUE (zheeg). A lively dance form usually in 6/8 or 12/8 meter.

GIOCOSO (joh KOH soh). To be performed in a playful or humorous fashion.

GRANDEZZA (grahn DEH tsah). Grandeur.

GRAZIOSO (grah stee OH zoh). In a graceful manner.

GROSSO (GROH soh). Grand, full, or great.

HARPSICHORD. A keyboard instrument which is shaped like a small grand piano but differs in the manner of tone production. The strings of the harpsichord are plucked rather than being struck by a hammer.

HOB. An abbreviation for the name, Anthony van Hoboken, a scholar who compiled a thematic catalog of the complete works by Haydn. All numbers correspond to the listings in this index.

INNIG (IN nikh). Heartfelt, fervent.

INNOCENT (EE noh tshent). In an artless and simple style.

INVENTION. A short keyboard composition in two-part counterpoint.

LÄNDLER (LEND lerr) A slow dance usually in 3/4 or 3/8 meter.

LARGHETTO (lahr GET toh). A tempo indication meaning to play slowly but not as slow as largo.

LARGO (LAHR goh). A tempo indication meaning to play very slowly.

LEBHAFT (LAYP hahft). An indication for a lively, vivacious tempo.

LEGATO (lay GAH toh). Instruction to provide a smooth connection of all notes.

LÉGER (lay zhay). Light, nimble.

LEGGIERO (lay JAY roh). Light, delicate.

LENTO (LEN toh). A slow tempo.

MA (mah). But.

MAESTOSO (mah ess TOH soh). To play in a dignified way, stately, majestic.

MARCATO (mar KAH toh). To accent the notes strongly, well pronounced.

MÄSSIG (MAY sihk). Moderate tempo.

MAZURKA (mah ZUR kah). A country dance that was popular in Poland during the eighteenth and nineteenth centuries. Chopin was one of the first to adapt the dance traits to concert music. Usually in 3/4 or 3/8 meter.

MENO (MAY noh). Less.

MESTO (MESS toh). Sad, mournful.

MEZZO (MED zoh). Medium, half. *Mezzo forte (mf)*, medium loud.

MINORE (mee NOH ray). Minor.

MINUET. A dance in 3/4 meter that was popular in France during the seventeenth century. Now appears in instrumental music as a complete work or movement of a large composition.

MISSA (MEE sah). A Mass.

MODERATO (moh dehr RAH toh). A moderate tempo. Also used to "moderate" a tempo, for example, *allegro moderato*: moderately fast.

MODÉRÉ (moh DAYR rai). Moderate tempo.

MOSSO (MOH soh). Motion, movement. *Meno mosso*, less movement, slower.

MOTO (MOH toh). Motion.

MUNTER (MOON terr). Lively.

MUSICAL. A light play set to music and comprised of solo songs, duets, choruses, dialogue, and usually dancing.

NON (nohn). Not, no.

OFFERTORIUM, OFFERTORY. A part of the Roman Catholic Mass. This follows the Credo and is the fourth of five items from the Proper of the Mass.

OPERA. A play set to music for solo voices, chorus, orchestra, and often dancers. Costumes, acting, dialogue, and scenery are very much a part of these productions.

ORATORIO. A large work written for vocal soloists, chorus, orchestra, and/or organ. Most oratorios are based on religious subjects and are structured similarly to the opera, except there is no staging, scenery, costumes, or dramatic action.

ORDINARIO, ORDINARY. The portions of the Catholic services which retain the same text throughout the church year.

OVERTURE. A portion of instrumental music preceding an opera or oratorio. Overtures have also been composed as one-movement concert pieces and are called *concert-overtures*.

PARTITA (par TEE tah). The term used for a composition of a suite or set of variations. *Partite* is the plural form.

PESANTE (pay ZAHN tay). Indicates that a passage or section should be played with a heavy and sustained tone.

PIACEVOLE (pee ah CHAY voh lay). Pleasantly, easily.

PIANO (pee AH noh). Soft; the abbreviation is *p*.

POCO (POH koh). A little, or somewhat. Used with other terms: *poco crescendo*, a little louder.

POMPOSO (pohm POH soh). Pompous, stately, or grand.

PRELUDE. A title used for a composition which precedes a fugue or opera or begins a suite. The term is also used for a self-contained composition.

PRESTO (PRAY stoh). Lively, quickly, rapidly.

QUARTET. A composition for four voices or instruments. The string quartet is comprised of two violins, one viola, and one cello. A vocal quartet consists of a soprano, alto, tenor, and bass.

QUASI (KWAH zee). As if, almost.

REQUIEM (RAY kwee yem). The Roman Catholic Mass for the dead. Many composers have composed elaborate settings of this liturgy. The term is based on the initial text, "Requiem aeternam dona eis Domine" (Grant them eternal rest, O Lord).

RITARDANDO (ree tahr DAHN doh). Becoming slower. Abbreviated as *rit.*, or *ritard.*

RONDO (RAHN doh). A musical form characterized by the alternation of a principal theme (section) with contrasting material, for example, A – B – A – B – A, A – B – A – C – A, or A – B – A – C – A – B – A.

ROUNDED BINARY. A musical form in two sections. Somewhat similar to binary form except for the return of the initial material toward the end of the second section — ‖ A ‖ B A ‖

SARABANDE (Fr.), SARABAND (Eng.). A slow dance in 3/2 or 3/4 meter. It originated in Spain and has become a standard part of the suite.

SCHERZANDO (skair TSAHN doh). Lively, playfully.

SCHERZOSO (skair TSOH zoh). Same as *scherzando*: lively, playfully.

SCHNELL (shnel). Fast.

SEMPLICE (SEM plee chay). Simple, simply.

SEMPRE (SEM pray). Always or continuing.

SIMPLE TERNARY. A musical form comprised of three sections: A – B – A.

SONATA (soh NAH tah). An important instrumental composition which contains three or four distinct movements, fast, slow, dancelike (omitted in some cases), and fast. This form is used not only for single instruments, such as piano sonata, violin sonata (violin with piano accompaniment), and flute sonata (flute with piano accompaniment), and so on, but also for a group of instruments. Although the basic form of the sonatas for various instrumental groupings is the same, the term used for these pieces differs: a sonata for orchestra, *symphony*; four strings, *string quartet*; three strings, *trio*; solo instrument with orchestral accompaniment, *concerto*.

SONATA – ALLEGRO (soh NAH tah – ahl LAY groh). A most significant musical form which is used in the first movement and may also be found in the second and fourth movements of sonatas, string quartets, symphonies, and so on. The structure of sonata–allegro form contains three large sections — exposition, development, and recapitulation — each of which subdivides into smaller components.

SOSTENUTO (soss teh NOO toh). An indication that notes should be sustained for the full duration, thus producing a smooth articulation.

SOTTO (SOH toh). Under, below.

SOTTO VOCE (VOH chay). Softly, in a low voice.

SPIRITO (SPEE ree toh). With spirit, energy.

STACCATO (stah KAH toh). Detached, with separation.

STRAFF (shtrahf). Rigid, strict.

SUBITO (SOO bee toh). Suddenly, immediately.

SUITE. A type of composition consisting of a series of movements in dance forms. Among the dance forms found in the Baroque suite are allemande, courante, sarabande; an optional use of minuet, bouree, gavotte, and so on; and finally the gigue.

SYMPHONY. A composition written for an orchestra in sonata form, that is, in four movements: fast, slow, dancelike (minuet or scherzo), and fast.

TRÈS (tray). Very, most.

TRIO. A composition for three instruments or three voices; *string trio*, violin, viola, and cello; *piano trio*, piano, violin, and cello. The term is also used in conjunction with the middle portion of a minuet or scherzo.

TROPPO (TROP poh). Too much. *Non troppo*: not too much.

UND (oont). And.

VALSE. Waltz.

VALZER (VAHL tser). Waltz.

VARIATIONS. A musical form which begins with a vivid statement of a theme in the opening section and is followed by a number of variations of this melody in the subsequent sections.

VIF (veef). Lively.

VIVACE (vee VAH chay). Animated, lively, briskly.

VIVO (VEE voh). Animated, briskly, lively.

VOCE (VOH chay). Voice.

WALTZ. A dance in 3/4 meter which became a popular instrumental form during the nineteenth century.

WELL-TEMPERED CLAVIER (klah VEER). Title of two sets of preludes and fugues for keyboard instruments written by Bach to demonstrate the advantages of *equal temperament*, a new tuning system which is still in use today.

ZART (tsart). Tender, delicate.